Power Failure

Power Failure

Christianity in the Culture
of Technology

Albert Borgmann

Brazos Press
A Division of Baker Book House Co
Grand Rapids, Michigan 49516

Copyright © 2003 by Albert Borgmann

Published by Brazos Press
A division of Baker Book House Company
P.O. Box 6287, Grand Rapids, MI 49516–6287
www.brazospress.com

Printed in the United States of America

Library of Congress Cataloging-in-Publication Data
Borgmann, Albert.
   Power Failure : Christianity in the culture of technology / Albert Borgmann.
       p.   cm.
   Includes bibliographical references.
   ISBN 1-58743-058-4 (pbk.)
   1. Religion and science. 2. Technology—Religious aspects—Christianity. I. Title.

BL240.3 B67 2003
261.5′6—dc21
                                                              2002152382

Contents■

Introduction   7

Part 1: The Circumstances of the Culture of Technology
1. The Invisibility of Contemporary Culture   11
2. The Moral Significance of Material Culture   25
3. Communities of Celebration   35

Part 2: The Place of Christianity in the Culture of Technology
4. Contingency and Grace   65
5. Power and Care   81
6. Liberty, Festivity, and Poverty   95
7. Courage and Fortitude   109
8. The Culture of the Word and the Culture of the Table   117

Notes   129
Index   139

5

Introduction ■

Those of us who live in the advanced industrial countries enjoy unprecedented liberty and prosperity. A crucial part of our freedom is political—the freedom of democracy. But what is truly novel and unique is the liberation we owe modern technology—freedom from hunger, cold, disease, ignorance, and confinement. Just as remarkable is the positive counterpart to liberation, namely, enrichment—the immense prosperity of goods and services that technology has delivered. We are doing very well.

But Christianity is not. All indications are that, as the standard of living rises, faith declines. The population of the richest among the first world countries shows the least belief in God and in life after death and has the lowest church attendance. It also seems that religious convictions decrease as the level of education increases.[1] This country is to some degree an exception, but church membership and church attendance in the United States have also been declining.[2] And here, too, the more affluent and better educated are less religious.[3]

Christianity is still the largest religion in the world and will likely remain so in the foreseeable future.[4] But its strength lies in the southern hemisphere, where Christianity is expanding, and that part of the world is less affluent and less educated in the academic sense than the northern half. This, too, suggests that there is a connection between the progress of technology and the decline of faith.

Technology, in this context, is meant to designate not just an ensemble of machines and procedures, but a type of culture, the kind that is characteristic of the advanced industrial societies and has been developing and gaining definition for two and a half centuries. The connection between technology and Christianity is troubling for two reasons. Most obviously the progress of technology seems to render Christianity superfluous and irrelevant. The good news of the Gospels is directed toward oppressed and poor people, one might think, and when oppression and poverty have been lifted by technology, the good news becomes old.

What is troubling as well is the fuzzy outline and uncertain force of technology and hence of the challenge Christianity is facing. What kind of liberation is it that technology has promised? What sort of riches has technology produced? Do we in fact feel free? Are we truly prospering? These questions go largely unasked in our national conversation. We seem to be stricken with a subclinical malady of doubt and sometimes despair. But in this second sort of trouble there lies hope as well. Perhaps underneath the surface of technological liberty and prosperity there is a sense of captivity and deprivation, and we may hope that once we understand technology more incisively and clearly, there will be good news once again.

That, at any rate, is the argument of the essays that follow. They have been published previously and severally and have been revised, coordinated, and arranged for this collection so that there is some cohesion and sequential order amongst them. They follow one another roughly in an order from the more general to the more particular and from the more preparatory to the more conclusive. The first three examine and expose crucial features of contemporary culture, some inimical to Christianity and some hospitable. Each of the following five investigates a particular linkage between technology and Christianity and in each case concludes with a positive Christian response to the challenge of technology.

These essays are broadly philosophical in character though there is very little of the technical terminology of contemporary philosophy—"philosophical" here means *reflective* and *reasoned*. Reason and reflection cannot presume to govern faith, but they can precede it and clear a space for it. Making room for Christianity is in fact the most promising response to technology. We should neither try to demolish technology nor run away from it. We can restrain it and must redeem it.

Part 1 ■

The Circumstances
of the Culture
of Technology

1

The Invisibility of Contemporary Culture

There are many cultures around the globe today. Among them the culture of the advanced industrial countries is surely the most distinctive. All other cultures, for better or worse, tend toward it. By contemporary culture I mean the technologically advanced style of life.

Contemporary culture is extremely conscious of itself. No prior culture has had so much information about itself, has taken its pulse so often, or has done so much talking about itself. And yet it seems to me that contemporary culture is essentially blind to itself. It is ignorant of its essential character. We can get a first indication of this concealment when we consider two privileged modes of discourse of contemporary culture, namely, scientific and political discourse.

It has become fashionable to emphasize the instability of scientific insight and to stress the kinship between the epistemologies of the sciences and the humanities. But this fashion ignores the progress and the cogency of science. Einstein has superseded Newton in a way in which Arthur Miller has failed to supersede Shakespeare. And Steven Weinberg's unified theory of the weak nuclear and electromagnetic forces won the kind of acceptance that John Rawls's theory of justice has never enjoyed. In the natural sciences there is always by near unan-

11

imous consent a best current theory. There never is any such thing in the humanities.

The privileged status of political discourse is less controversial. Its privilege consists not in its cogency or progressiveness but in its overpowering presence. Scientific discourse has the strongest claim on our assent, political discourse on our attention. Politics occupies the front page of the newspapers and first place in the newscasts. But neither kind of discourse speaks about the character of our culture. As an example of scientific discourse, consider the 2001 issues of *Scientific American*. Here we find science speaking with unchallenged authority about the nature of the very large ("Echoes from the Big Bang," "Making Sense of Modern Cosmology") and about the structure of the very small ("Photonic Crystals," "100 Years of Quantum Mysteries").[1] When it turns to the middle-sized realm in which we enact our culture, natural science must, if it wants to speak cogently, confine itself to fairly limited aspects ("Genetically Modified Foods: Are They Safe?" "Safeguarding Our Water"). The focus of natural science, we might say, sweeps past the texture and flavor of our daily lives.

In politics we take comprehensive responsibility for the vast machinery that supports our daily lives. We attend to its energy and resource requirements, to its domestic safety and global security, and to the economy and tranquility of its administration. Accordingly, the *New York Times* on the front page of its 24 March 2002 issue reported on the genesis of the Bush administration's national energy report, on the turmoil in the Mideast, on the lack of security in small town banks, among other things. However, the nature and the value of the life that consumes energy and proceeds within whatever margins of security— this central and crucial area of the common order remains occluded in political discourse.

It is a simple fact that philosophy as a professional discipline commands neither assent nor attention. When Anglo-American philosophers contemplate the state of their art, they readily concede the lack of consensus within their profession and the indifference of the culture at large to the profession itself.[2] At the same time there is no denying the extreme rigor and precision of contemporary philosophical work, which gives the impression that all the finely wrought philosophical pieces are destined eventually to fit together into a compelling, imposing, and intricate structure. But one will search in vain for the emerging outlines of such an edifice.

As regards the flavor and texture of our historical situation, its center of gravity, and its deepest hopes and fears, readers of contemporary philosophy would have to rely on fragments, allusions, and asides. If beyond that they would conjecture, on the basis of philosophy alone, about the character of a culture that had begotten this kind of philosophy, what would they gather? They might think that the general and preliminary character of philosophy was the reflection of an unsettled and preliminary culture, one that had not yet attained a forceful and enduring shape and therefore did neither permit a concrete description and sustained critique nor inspire a definite counterproposal. As we know, that conjecture would be entirely mistaken. The advanced industrial culture at the beginning of the twenty-first century is both the cause and the result of the most radical transformation of the planet in human history.

Though philosophy, science, and politics are blind to the character of contemporary culture, they are implicated in it just the same. Philosophers live by the grace of the present culture. They are supported and suffered, but not understood or appreciated, by those who produce affluence and wield power today. Mainstream philosophers, on their part, at least in this country, have been little concerned to clarify the terms on which they work in, with, or against society. At the same time, it seems to me, Anglo-American philosophers are in competition with contemporary culture. No engineer, no tool and die maker could be more concerned to design and work up objects of such precision and polish. It is of course conceptual structures that are fashioned in this way. And they are intended not to solve this or that particular problem of daily life but to reconstitute such fundamental issues as existence, knowledge, language, intelligence, emotion, action, and ethical conduct. Once completed, these precise and gleaming structures, so one assumes, will improve the human lot much more powerfully than the invention of Cool Whip, cars, or television has done.

The implication of natural science in the present common order is more straightforward. Natural science can be seen as a contemplative enterprise, devoted to discovering and understanding the lawful order of reality. However, it is not the intrinsically ennobling force of penetrating knowledge for which science is valued in our society, but the technologically transformative power that lies in such knowledge. *Scientific American* traces the course of the exercise of that power to a certain extent. It contains articles on "Arctic Oil and the Wildlife Refuge" and on "The Science of Persuasion."[3] But it resolutely ignores the terminal area where energy consumption, the use of manufactured goods, and all economic efforts find their end and justification, i.e., the area of final consumption.

The situation is similar in politics. It may be thought that cultural and moral concerns asserted themselves in the election of George W. Bush as president. But at bottom it is the advancement of economic well-being that determines whether a politician's career lives or dies. To speak of "the advancement of economic well-being" is to use the polite political language that refrains from examining and even from acknowledging the final consumptive purposes that govern our government.

The concealment of the heart of contemporary culture has many more aspects, and it is not nearly as tight in social studies and modern fiction as it is in standard philosophy, science, and politics. In fact comprehensive and profound critiques of contemporary American culture have been provided by sociologists and theologians. But clearly the difficulty and magnitude of this enterprise require that others join in the task. "Philosophy of technology" is, I believe, an appropriate title and directive for a crucial part of such a cooperative venture. "Technology" properly directs us to those concrete quotidian structures in which we act out our hopes and frustrations both inconspicuously and decisively. This level of contemporary existence is too often overlooked; and as long as it is, we will have a distorted or incomplete view of the character of today's common order.

To work out a clear and comprehensive view of the world and of our place in it has always been the task of philosophy. In this sense, the philosophy of technology is a traditional enterprise. But the tradition of philosophy has throughout been redefined by its leading concern. In the philosophy of technology that redefinition is likely to be more risky and radical than it has been for some time. The problem is that technology in the required theoretical sense fails to have the rather clear pretheoretical articulation that is proper to science or to politics. In the philosophy of technology the problem will only be clear once the solution has been presented. "Technology" helpfully gathers intuitions and experiences for this task; but it would be a mistake to expect more from this term and to act as though nothing more than persistent surveying and sorting were needed to discover underneath it as clear and articulate an object of inquiry as science or politics. Hence antecedent considerations such as the foregoing ones that attempt to delimit and secure its subject matter in advance are of limited value in the philosophy of technology. It is finally a matter of proposing concrete observations and suggestions about the decisive pattern of our lives.

14

Let me sketch, then, one way of taking up with the philosophy of technology.[4] To grasp the inconspicuous and elusive quotidianity of the technological culture, consider Cool Whip. It is a nondairy whipped topping. This labored generic description for what is simply artificial whipped cream bespeaks a residual uneasiness in our habits of replacing natural or traditional things with technologically reconstituted items. In practice, the scruples matter little. When Cool Whip tops your cake, you can hardly tell it from whipped cream. It has very nearly the color, consistency, and taste of whipped and sweetened cream.[5] All this seems plain enough, too plain in fact to engage philosophical reflection. So to make the contours of technological dailiness come into relief, consider a recipe with the following ingredients:

> Water, hydrogenated coconut and palm kernel oils, corn syrup, sugar, sodium caseinate, dextrose, polysorbate 60, natural and artificial flavors, sorbitan monostearate, xanthan gum and guar gum. Artificial color.

What would you come up with if you combined these ingredients in the right amounts and in the right way and used the right flavors and colors? It might be illegal to try since you could be in violation of United States patent number 3431117, held by General Foods. As you will have guessed, the patent contains the formula for Cool Whip.[6] But had the description of the underlying structure of Cool Whip not followed so closely on the description of the surface appearance of Cool Whip, the inference from one to the other would have been impossible for nearly everyone.

To be sure, if a chemical analysis of the traditional thing were given, most people would not recognize cream in it either. Still, cream even now is woven into the texture and depth of our world in a way in which Cool Whip can never be. Skimming off cream is taking and keeping the best. Cream rises to the top. It is the cream of the crop, la crème de la crème. Think of peaches and cream and of all the creamy things you have tasted. Here is Robert Farrar Capon's song in praise of cream:

> And but me no buts about the cream, especially if you can still buy unhomogenized milk. To be sure, those who are utterly at the mercy of the supermarket will be forced to buy their cream straight, or in the slightly dishonest form of half and half. But if you can get plain milk with cream floating on top, you are practically guaranteed a reputation as a cook. To begin with, your children will normally hate the cream; therefore you can skim every quart of milk you use. Second, you can get cream of any desired weight by skimming lightly or deeply. And third, you can splash

it about with a lavish hand. Fried anything can be treated to a little top of the bottle with no examination of conscience whatsoever. Once again, it is a time to be rich enough—or poor enough—to play. You have nothing to lose but your homogenized chains.[7]

Cool Whip in comparison is an opaque article. Its origin and substructure are concealed by a vague and implicit understanding of anonymous research and development scientists, of Food and Drug Administration regulations, of distant factories, and of supermarket chains. If coconut oil were replaced by cottonseed oil, dextrose by aspartame, and one emulsifier by another, we would hardly notice. Why then do people exchange Cool Whip for whipped cream? Cool Whip is cheaper than cream; it is already whipped and stays so for two weeks if stored in a refrigerator; and, important in an affluent society, it has no cholesterol and fewer calories, only 14 per serving. All these attractive features can be gathered under the notion of availability. Cool Whip is more available than whipped cream. And if changes in the substructure of Cool Whip should take place as suggested above, they will affect Cool Whip only by making it more available yet, i.e., cheaper, more durable, less fattening.

But does anything of philosophical moment turn on the fact that in some cases a traditional, contextual thing has been replaced by an article that is opaque and more available? Yes, insofar as the case of Cool Whip exhibits a pattern that is pervasive in an advanced industrial society. Nearly everything that surrounds a citizen of such a society exhibits the opaque and commodious availability of Cool Whip and rests on a sophisticated and unintelligible machinery. All of our foods, our clothing, shelter, implements, and entertainment are of that character. It is an instructive exercise to take any of these ordinary items and to work out its analogy with Cool Whip. The analogy comes out more sharply the more clearly and comprehensively we set the item in its historical context, i.e., against the traditional things it has replaced and against the more advanced devices by which it will be overtaken some day. Some such a replacement is always taking place in the progress of technology, no matter how unprecedented the invention. For human life at any one time is full and complete. It never contains empty slots that await the insertion of a novel commodity. A technological novelty will take its place in our lives when we have discarded something old to make room for the new.

Consider the contrast that Dorothy Hartley has drawn between the technological universe of opaque surfaces and an older time when things disclosed a deeper world:

> A modern woman sees a piece of linen, but the mediaeval woman saw through it to the flax fields, she smelt the reek of the retting ponds, she felt the hard rasp of the hackling, and she saw the soft sheen of the glossy flax. Man did not just see "leather," he saw the beast—perhaps one of his own—and knew the effort of slaughtering, liming and curing.[8]

Of course our culture is even less perspicuous than the modern world Hartley envisages. Linen has been replaced by cotton and polyester blends, and leather by plastics.

Even if the pattern of Cool Whip is seen in all the technological devices and implements that surround us, the most troubling extension of it is yet to be recognized. The availability, the freshness, the uniform perfection, and the absence of demands that we value in Cool Whip we seek in persons as well, and being aware of how widely Cool Whip persons are appreciated, we seek to restyle ourselves in that image. Accordingly, as we remake our personality and appearance to lend them the appeal of availability, we foreshorten our existence into an opaque, if glamorous, surface and replace the depth of tradition and rootedness of life by a concealed and intricate machinery of techniques and therapies.

What we are seeing here is not an accomplished fact but a tendency that asserts itself, and is resisted, in varied and ambiguous ways. In fact, thoughtful reflections on technology are typically haunted by ambiguity and ambivalence. The challenge here is to avoid both premature resolutions and endless impressionism. The challenge can be met by fixing and clarifying our impressions through the articulation of appropriate conceptual structures. I have earlier complained about the devotion of Anglo-American mainstream philosophers to precision and cogency and asserted that this penchant puts them in competition with technology. Am I not falling into the same trap in reaching for conceptual structures? My reply is that conceptual articulation is indeed congenial to technology. It can serve to heighten and expose the character of technology. Once it is exposed, we can hope to overcome it through a kind of discourse in which concepts become secondary.

At any rate I propose to call the distinctive surface appearance of technological items the commodity to reflect the commodious and tradable availability of such items. The concealed deep structure on which commodities rest and depend I call the machinery to designate the debt that commodity owes to science and engineering. The compound of commodity and machinery is the (technological) device. The distinctive pattern of the division and connection of its components is the device paradigm.

This conceptual structure invites four kinds of extensions and elaborations. (1) The most obvious is the conceptual and structural elaboration, the articulation of finer features and variant types. This elaboration must take its guidance from two further extensions. (2) The first of these is the (naively) phenomenological elaboration of the pattern that consists in testing it against the most varied and recalcitrant technological phenomena, from the smallest, like silicon chips, to the largest, such as the interstate highway system; from the tangible, such as a highrise building, to the conceptual, like a legal contract; from the obvious, like an automobile, to the unsuspected, such as a suburban lawn; from the structural, such as a bridge, to the organizational, such as the insurance industry. The phenomenological extension allows one to appreciate and to draw on the stimulating if scattered and inconclusive observations of the contemporary culture that one finds in fiction, in films, and occasionally in the columns of our prominent pundits. (3) Next the conceptual structure of the device paradigm invites us to extend it into a discussion of scholarship, both of methods and of substantive positions. It leads us to the question of what kind of explanation is attempted here and what kind of evidence will tell for or against one's claims. This extension of the device paradigm connects up with the lively contemporary discussions about deconstructionism, holism, and hermeneutics. When one raises the substantive question regarding the standing that the device paradigm has in the collective awareness and in the common order, one enters into a conversation, and often into a controversy, with the major social philosophies: liberalism, conservatism, communitarianism, and Marxism.

All of these extensions and elaborations depend on (4) the final extension of the device paradigm. I mean final in two senses. The first is the straightforwardly extensive sense. We must ask what the expansion and intensification of the rule, i.e., of the dominant cultural force, of technology will tell us about the character of technology, whether such an extension will finally resolve the tacit ambivalence that we feel about technology. In another sense, to turn to the final extension of the device paradigm is to extend the discussion of technology to the question of ends, to the moral salience of the device paradigm, and to the religious challenge that technology poses for us.

Let me leave the first three extensions aside and attend to the final extension of the device paradigm. To begin with the straightforward expansion of technology, it is the hope of both advocates and critics that a dramatic enlargement of the rule of technology will disclose its secular significance. The advocates believe that the technological enterprise has yet to reach its full flowering, that technological invention will procure unprecedented prosperity and liberty, and that in the fullness of time technology will disclose to every reasonable person its overwhelmingly beneficial and gratifying character. Every technological innovation is hailed as the final stride toward that universally rich and satisfying life.

The critics of technology anticipate the expansion of technology with a grim sort of satisfaction. The moral or ecological debility that they now believe lies concealed at the heart of technology will then, they are confident, become incontrovertibly evident to everyone. The evidence, it is thought, will be some sort of manifest breakdown like social chaos or environmental catastrophe.

Both views, I believe, are mistaken. The progress of technology, once its basic pattern is seen, has had a numbing sameness for at least a century. There is nothing in the most recent innovations and prospects that falls outside of the pattern of technology. To be sure, the progress of technology produces ever greater refinements and ever more variations within the device paradigm. To the essential stagnation of technology there corresponds an amazingly resourceful stability. Cool Whip is in obvious ways a safer article than whipped cream. Since it needs no whipping, it never turns into butter or fails to get stiff; it does not turn sour nor does it clog your arteries. Safety is a component of availability; in pursuing the latter, technology procures the former. Of course, this is one tendency in technology that most everyone would wish to be stronger. On the other hand, the risks and dangers of technology are not among the invisible features of our culture. The discourse of science and politics is well able to attend to them. And so the optimism of those who are hoping that the expansion of technology will disclose its limits and liabilities with finality is unwarranted.

It is unlikely, then, that the simply extensive dynamics of the pattern of technology will in due course disclose the moral character of technology for better or worse. The lesson to be learned here is that contemporary culture will not step out of its concealment when challenged by the conventional vocables of benefits and harms. Yet the moral complexion of technology is being advertised openly. In fact advertise-

19

ment is the mode of discourse that surpasses scientific and political discourse in glamour and prominence.

Ironically, the singular visibility and power that advertisement has been given by contemporary culture go along with an equally widespread sense of embarrassment and contempt at the frivolous or incredible claims of so many advertisements. Scholars are divided on how we are to explain this phenomenon; not surprisingly, philosophers have for the most part stayed aloof from this mundane problem.

Although the status of advertisement in our culture is confused, the message of advertising is clear. Advertisers present as vividly and seductively as possible life among the most refined commodities. It is a life of unchallenged power and glorious comfort. There has been a shift in the style of advertisements within the last two decades although the message has remained the same. In 1985, advertisements were garrulous. Thus the transatlantic traveler was familiarly addressed in second person singular. "Say, for example," said TWA, you're traveling across the Atlantic.

> TWA is introducing a 747 Business Class seat that makes all others obsolete. Our new Business Lounger tilts to cradle you in comfort. The foot rest adjusts to your height. And it's the widest seat in the sky.[9]

If lounging your way across the Atlantic was not comfortable enough, you could sleep your way across it as well.

> We often have a leg up on the competition. And our First Class Sleeper Seat is no exception. On every TWA widebody, you can stretch out the length of four windows. Put your feet up. And relax in a wealth of space.[10]

Back on earth, one's command of time and space, of wind and weather was rendered similarly complete. If you were a tenant of the then Pan Am Building, you could take the subway from the airport to New York's railroad and subway hub, and walk directly from there to your office. The advertisement went to some length in laying the kingdom of technological power and comfort at your feet.

> Walk unencumbered from your train through Grand Central Terminal into one of New York's most celebrated buildings. Cross the lobby and step onto one of the 59 high speed elevators. Maximum wait: 12 seconds. Upon reaching your floor, your key unlocks not only your office door but a wealth of amenities offered through our Executive Services Director. His sole responsibility is your special business needs. Like limousines,

theatre tickets or teleconferencing. He can serve as your catering coordinator for almost any kind of function. So if your company is considering a move, call Cross & Brow Company, at 212-986-2100. And see what makes the Pan Am Building such a civilized work environment. Especially on rainy days.[11]

More recently, advertisements have been chiefly alluring pictures with a surprising angle—a gleaming sports coupe racing through a blurred landscape (Acura); the hands and legs of a yuppie couple playing dominoes by the pool (Cole Haan); three strikingly radiant women, sitting on granite blocks (Eileen Fisher).[12]

The significance of such advertisements lies in their normative force. They exhibit the norms of the technological way of life, the allure of commodious power in its most advanced refinement. They do not literally describe or offer a common way of life. Of the millions of readers of the *New York Times Magazine*, a few hundred will traverse the Atlantic in Sleeper Seats and only a few dozen had cause to call 212-986-2100. But most of the millions of readers have aspirations that are oriented and articulated by the standards that are here so skillfully and prominently exemplified.

The dubious standing of advertising in our society is already an indication of a certain liability in the normative pattern of technology. That same instability is apparent in the advertisements themselves. Being asleep for six hours and, on awakening, finding oneself on the other side of the Atlantic are not by themselves animating or invigorating activities. But they are pleasant affairs, tinged with feelings of relief and perhaps even triumph if previously one had to spend six sleepless nocturnal hours in a cramped and confining seat. Similarly, to drive a coupe or to walk through covered spaces is exciting only if normally you would have to struggle through rainy and windy conditions.

There is at least a drowsy and perhaps even a dawning sense in the contemporary culture that the paradigmatic blessings of technology are vacuous. I am not speaking of the genuine constructive technological accomplishments of liberating people from hunger, disease, illiteracy, and backbreaking work. What is beginning to appear dubious is rather the value of those efforts that are dedicated to extending the limits of availability. To the air travelers, the night sky has become an abstraction. The wealth of space that they enjoy is simply room for their legs and arms. For the business executive, an "Executive Services Director" is no more a trusted friend and helper than an automatic door opener. Driving a car is not really an event that provokes us to shouts of "Wow!"

21

and "Sweet!"[13] It is the parasitic vacuity at the center of the technological culture that the philosophy of technology must examine and expose. The recognition of this unhappy voraciousness naturally shades over into a concern for what technology continues to devour and displace. Philosophers, like many citizens of the technological society, may be privately sensitive to the dignity of vanishing things and practices and feel sorrow at their disappearance or destruction. But philosophy as a professional discipline is not well equipped to give voice and public force to these sentiments.

The discipline of precision and incisiveness that philosophy has cultivated for so long lends itself well to a critique of technology. It can even initiate the turn from critique to advocacy. It can demonstrate that there is an essential, as opposed to a merely extensive, limit to technology, the latter understood as the procurement and consumption of commodities. That limit consists in what is essentially unprocurable, those things and practices that exist in their own right and must be met with engagement and respect if they are to disclose their identity. These things and practices may have commodious counterparts in technology, and the commodities may even bear the same name as their pretechnological correlates. As it happens, the Food and Drug Administration does not allow Cool Whip to be called "whipped cream." But we naturally call "traveling" what amounts to being transported in an airplane's Sleeper Seat although this mode of transport differs more radically from the traditional travail of traversing and appropriating space than Cool Whip differs from traditional whipped cream.

We can further, in the common philosophical manner, conceptually distinguish these unprocurable phenomena as focal things and practices to indicate how they gather our world and radiate significance in ways that contrast with the diversion and distraction afforded by commodities. We can even specify the generic traits that the various focal things and practices share to show how vigorous and broadly based, if officially ignored, the focal culture is in this country.

Focal things and practices are the crucial counterforces to technology understood as a form of culture. They contrast with technology without denying it, and they provide a standpoint for a principled and fruitful reform of technology. Generally, a focal thing is concrete and of commanding presence. A focal practice is the decided, regular, and normally communal devotion to a focal thing.

22

But in the end such definitions are but promissory notes that are redeemed when we are able to speak eloquently on behalf of the thing and the practice that focus our life. Not every philosopher has the gift of that eloquence. Happily, neither does the burden of such speaking fall primarily on philosophers. There are already poets, writers, and people of practical wisdom who have spoken powerfully for their focal concerns. In fact one of the issues of the *New York Times Magazine* that featured the advertisements of technological glamour also contained a wonderful testimony by Benjamin DeMott on his focal concern, "Hanging Out with Horses."[14]

His horse, Terence, centers and discloses for DeMott the depth and power of the world, "the immense snowy stillness after a storm" and the "joy when the world suddenly decides to talk back. The scary no-warning swerve of a horse spooked by grouse that the rider failed to notice behind yonder wall." For DeMott, a critic and novelist, deconstructionism is the learned counterpart of the technological assembling and reassembling of opaque surfaces, an ensemble that is about to close in on itself and behind all these surfaces appears to contain nothing but more surfaces. How is one to reply to the deconstructionist? "Sir. I refute you thus, says Terence in his cross ties, producing a fresh pile of dung for the edification of the barn floor."

Love of horses lends substance to DeMott's family relations. It is the focus of his hopes for his grandson, James, and a bond of affection to his father with whom otherwise he "fought plenty." Love of horses connects him to places in Colorado and England with an intimacy that tourism could never afford. And love of horses stills his "hunger for physicality," his desire to be bodily in touch with the world and to have the bodily strength needed to do so. Throughout the essay there is the less direct and yet pervasive and appreciative celebration of the horse itself, of that magnificent and now altogether useless creature in whose creation humans and nature have wonderfully cooperated.

The moral limitation and desiccation of technology do not come fully into view until they are seen against the vitality and humor of a focal practice. But focal concerns on their part live in hiding and at the margins of the official technological culture. DeMott speaks of his focal practice as the "love of truancy." "Truancy" conveys well the uncertain and marginal position that focal things and practices occupy. But it also carries the promise of a genuinely free and leisurely engagement with the world.[15] This is what DeMott rightly loves.

Accordingly, the philosophy of technology must become the love of truancy. Some of the best in contemporary moral philosophy has been moved by a similar aspiration, by the recognition of how arid the pursuit of general and abstract moral principles is and by the turn to the eloquent particularity of the world.[16] But truancy and aspiration must both mature into something more settled and substantial. We must work to move focal concerns from the outside to the center of the contemporary culture and allow the truants to become celebrants of the things and practices that finally matter.

What stands in the way of such a reform is not so much a lack of good will as a misconception about ethics. Most people, when prompted, would agree with mainstream philosophers that the right ethical theory will guide us to the good life and that the crucial moral problem is to discover which theory is correct. But this is half right at best. The factor that most decisively channels the daily course of life is not moral theory but material culture.

2 ■

The Moral Significance of Material Culture

Modern philosophy has been at two removes from the real world. First, in aspiring to theory, it has been distanced from practice. Theory can inform practice, but practice is richer than theory and, above all, self-sustaining. Practice can survive without theory while theory arises from a practice and perishes without the nourishment of a practice. Practice, as philosophers have always seen it, is in turn removed from its tangible setting. Yet material culture constrains and details practice decisively. Practice, abstracted from its tangible circumstances, is reduced to gesturing and sometimes to posturing.

Philosophy as we know it began with Plato, and in the beginning material reality was thought to be the adversary and seducer of philosophy. To philosophize was to rise above the tangible phenomena to the intelligible ideas. And while Aristotle acknowledged the life of pleasure and the life of honor and action, it is the life of contemplation that constitutes human fulfillment. Contemplation in Greek is *theoria;* with Aristotle, the word and the vision that were to rule philosophy came to the fore. They continued their reign through the Middle Ages, when the *vita contemplativa* was considered superior to the *vita activa.*

Practice, to be sure, was never far from ancient and medieval theory. To know the good is to do the good, says Plato. Virtue, says Aristotle, is a skilled practice. The 119 metaphysical questions of Thomas Aquinas's *Summa Theologica* are followed by 303 questions on ethics, 189 of them on virtues. Still, practice was always in the shadow of theory. Why? Practice, for the ancients and medievals, was enacted on a solid and familiar stage. Nature presented the powerful and regular backdrop of human life. Material culture presented a similarly firm and surveyable precinct. Where it changed, it did so, within any two or three generations, slowly and only in part. Not that the ancients and medievals were entirely unconcerned about the material world. They worried that it might provoke recklessness in the way humans shape it to their purposes and extravagance in the way they enjoy it. But all in all they took the material culture to be so solid and familiar that its direct bearing on philosophy could be handled in parentheses and asides.[1] Where moral virtues, chiefly temperance, referred to material goods, the solidity and familiarity of the latter authorized philosophers simply to presuppose them and to concentrate attention on the former.

Philosophical theory underwent a radical transformation at the beginning of the modern era. The most consequential development was the emigration and emancipation of the theory of nature from philosophy, a development that resulted in modern science.[2] From the start, beginning with Descartes and Bacon, natural science had for one of its objects the transformation of material nature for the liberation and enrichment of human life. The realization of this program was slow in coming, but it had an overpowering effect on philosophy. The effect was twofold. For one thing, philosophers without question accepted the scientific characterization of the fundamental transformation of material culture that was to result from scientific research. It would be the fulfillment of a promise of liberty and prosperity. Who would think of advocating servitude and poverty instead? For another, philosophers assimilated their enterprise to science but sought to execute it at a higher level. If science was to furnish a theory that would lead to an enlightened reconstruction of the physical environment, philosophy would provide a theory that was to bring about a salutary reconstruction of reality entire, including not only science and its subject, but also art, religion, politics, knowledge, and human conduct.

This then was the course of events that, in the modern period, removed philosophy from human practice and material culture. The latter was surrendered to science for illumination and transformation. The former was subjected to the reconstructive ambition of philosophical theory and ceased to be a subject of reflection in its own right.

While science by way of technology realized a certain version of its epochal project, the ambitions of philosophical theory became ever more marginal to modern society.[3] It was the pretentious poverty of theory that led Heidegger in 1927 and Oakeshott in the 1950s to reconsider and rehabilitate the dignity of practice.[4] Meanwhile feminism and post-modern particularism have attacked universal theory on a broad front and have delineated, elucidated, and recounted a great variety of human practices. All this is part of a commendable endeavor to recover the richness of life, to acknowledge the fragility and contingency of human circumstances, and to encourage the gentler voices in the conversation of humanity.

But if at its postmodern dawn philosophy has returned to practice, it has remained distant from material culture. The ontological enterprise, i.e., the endeavor to provide a philosophical theory that would illuminate the dark regions and clarify the confusions of all of reality, including material reality, has been stalemated.[5] Aesthetics does attend to the material embodiment of art, and it has begun its journey back to the fork where it parted ways with ethics.[6] Still, these efforts are too limited and tentative to cast much light on the moral charge of material culture. A similar limitation holds for the close historical studies of material culture one finds in journals such as *Technology and Culture* and *Material Culture*. If there is an implicit ethics in such studies, it is still the Enlightenment morality that vaguely applauds liberty, prosperity, and diversity.

Liberal and Marxist political philosophy has been keenly alert to the ethical significance of the distribution of material goods. But all color, texture, and flavor has been bleached from material culture. It has been reduced to one aspect, namely, of power. The distribution of goods is taken to be crucially and finally a distribution of power. The commendable goal of leftist analysis is equality or at least more of it. But the poverty of reducing material culture to power relations comes to the fore when Marx or Rawls contemplates the human condition once (greater) equality is achieved. What remains as the challenge of the good life is a bland and insubstantial notion of self-realization.[7]

A similar reductionism emerges when anthropologist Mary Douglas and economist Baron Isherwood consider *The World of Goods*.[8] Goods are reduced to information of which people possess more or less. They use it to communicate to one another their social standing; throughout the different social ranks, power once more is the spine of the body politic.[9] Still, Douglas and Isherwood belong to a loosely distinguishable group of social theorists and cultural critics who have been struck by the novel and troubling character of the material culture in the advanced industrial countries and have illuminated this issue in various ways.[10] But none dares to proceed to an explicit moral assessment. That is left to the professional moralists, the philosophers. Thus the moral significance of the material culture falls between the stools of the professions.

In at least one case, however, a sociological analysis of an important segment of our material setting, the home, leads right up to and some ways into a moral examination. Equally important, sociologists Mihaly Csikszentmihalyi and Eugene Rochberg-Halton remark expressly on how little is known about *The Meaning of Things*.[11] Lifting the veil of inconsiderability, the authors uncover what I take to be the crucial issue in the study of material culture.

It is a distinction between two kinds of things or reality. The first constitutes globally "a universe that speaks to humans."[12] Locally it comes to the fore in any object that conveys "meaning through its own inherent qualities" and through "the active contribution of the thing itself to the meaning process."[13] It is a kind of reality, however, that the authors find to be rarely acknowledged in their extensive interviews. Things are largely treated as semantically pliable material whose significance is shaped through an investment of psychic energy. There is much leeway for the emotional and moral shape a certain thing can be given.[14]

Let me call these two kinds of things and reality commanding reality and pliable or disposable reality. The latter kind is not unstructured, of course. We know as much from our command of common-sense distinctions. Nor is it intuitively obvious or trivial what kinds of things people especially endow with value in their homes.[15] But for an understanding of the moral salience of the material culture, Csikszentmihalyi and Rochberg-Halton's key finding is as important as it is disappointing—of itself material culture does not seem to matter much one way or another. They discovered two kinds of families, one they called "warm" and another they called "cool." Warm families talked about themselves in affectionate and positive terms while cool families described themselves and their concerns in neutral and guarded ways. Moreover, the two types of families exhibited strikingly different syndromes of goals, participation in the public sphere, and choice of role models and personality patterns, and yet "the kinds of objects mentioned by the two groups were essentially the same. . . . What did separate the two groups was simply the interpersonal meaning associated with the objects."[16]

Yet this disappointment rests on the assumption that the eclipse of commanding reality and the prominence of disposable reality as the nor-

28

mal arena of human conduct is itself morally inconsiderable. To raise the issue, consider music as an instance where the decline of commanding and the prominence of disposable reality comes into focus. In Csikszentmihalyi and Rochberg-Halton's study, music is considered under the headings of musical instruments and stereos.

A traditional musical instrument is surely a commanding thing. It is such simply as a physical entity, finely crafted of wood or metal, embodying centuries of development and refinement, sometimes showing the very traces of its service to many generations. An instrument particularly commands the attention of the student who, unless she is a prodigy, must through endless and painstaking practice adjust her body to the exacting requirements of this eminently sensitive thing. She must, moreover, train her eyes to read the music and her mind to transpose the visual information rapidly and easily into those bodily maneuvers the instrument will register. Music performed on an instrument in our presence captures our attention, and not only our ears but our eyes as well. We see the strings vibrate, the wood resonate, and the metal shape the sounding air. And the instrument, while it produces sound, reveals a person too, the grace or the strain or the fervor of the one who plays the instrument.

A stereo produces music as well or, in fact, much better, i.e., with the supernatural sonority and consistency that no live performance can sustain and with a range in the kinds of music that would require a standing army of virtuosi and virtuosae were it to be humanly available to a listener's call and beckon. Is a stereo a commanding piece of reality? As a physical entity, some sets are imposing in their size and high-tech gleam. Yet some stereos are praised for their slender and self-effacing physical appearance. As a thing to be operated, a stereo is certainly not demanding. Nor do we feel indebted to its presence the way we do when we listen to a musician. We respect a musician, we own a stereo. A set and the music it produces are entirely at our disposal.

In Csikszentmihalyi and Rochberg-Halton's research, instruments are mentioned as often as stereos among the objects people most cherish in their homes. Stereos and instruments rank fifth and sixth after furniture, visual art, photographs, and books.[17] But to cherish an object is one thing, to use it another. It is apparent from Csikszentmihalyi and Rochberg-Halton's discussion that people cherish stereos because they use and depend on them while an instrument is often valued as "a central symbol of a life-style once cherished or anticipated in the future."[18] Studies of how people in this country typically spend their time confirm these indications and our general intuition that musical instruments are rarely played in American homes, on the average three minutes or so a week, a seventh or eighth of the time that is spent on listening to recorded music.[19]

The case of music, then, instantiates the eclipse of commanding reality. It also affords the clues as to why and how this is happening, the why and the how being tightly connected. Why is recorded music preferred to performed music? The latter is arduous to master and limited in its range. But a complaint about such defects can become consequential only when there is a way of providing music effortlessly and abundantly. The history of the technology of recorded music is the history of obliging ever more fully the complaint about the burden and confinement of live music. Or to put the development more positively, at the beginning of the invention of recorded music stands a promise of disburdenment and enrichment, the promise to provide music freely and abundantly. This promise in turn is part of a larger one, namely, the promise of general liberty and prosperity—the promise that inaugurated the modern era.

In a democracy, such a promise cannot in principle be extended to a few and fulfilled through the servitude of the many. The task of furnishing a desirable good must be given over to a piece of machinery. In 1876, Thomas A. Edison rigged up a cylinder covered with a metal foil on which a stylus, activated by the vibrations of a membrane, inscribed a wavy groove as the cylinder turned. The membrane in turn moved in response to the sound waves of voices or instruments. The grooved recording on the cylinder could be played back by turning the cylinder and having another stylus follow the groove and activate a membrane.[20] From this machine the contemporary stereo has descended through innumerable ingenious mutations.

An Edison phonograph has an engaging simplicity and intelligibility. The voice moves the membrane, the membrane moves the stylus, the stylus grooves the metal foil and leaves a record. Reversing the process, we begin with the record and end with the sound. To be sure, it is hard for the layperson to appreciate that the richness and complexity of an orchestra can be reduced, for monaural purposes, to a single two-dimensional wave form and that ear and brain are capable of resolving that one compound waveform into the several components that represent the individual instruments. Yet the unintelligible residue of the Edison phonograph is limited and understandable as an articulate and limited problem if not as regards its solution.

The simplicity of the machinery corresponds of course to the crudeness of the commodity it produces. A simple phonograph produces poor sound. Correspondingly, today's stereo, which produces preternaturally perfect sound, is totally unintelligible to the typical consumer who does not even begin to understand the mathematics, logic, electronics, and mechanics that are embodied in a compact disc player and its associated equipment. As a consequence, music has become a disembodied, free-floating something, a commodity that is instantly, ubiquitously, and easily available.

Music has been mechanized and commodified. These two processes are really one. Music can become available as a cultural commodity only if there is a sophisticated and reliable machinery that will produce it at the consumer's will. I have called the conjunction of machinery and commodity a technological device. The stereo as a device contrasts with the instrument as a thing. A thing, in the sense in which I want to use the term, has an intelligible and accessible character and calls forth skilled and active human engagement. A thing requires practice while a device invites consumption. All this amounts to an explication of the distinction of realities derived from Csikszentmihalyi and Rochberg-Halton. Things constitute commanding reality, devices procure disposable reality.

If we inspect the typical American home from a historical perspective and with a view to its balance of things and devices, it becomes obvious that devices and consumption have replaced things and practices. Consider the culture of the table. The practice of cooking has been greatly diminished through the availability of convenience foods and microwave ovens. The practice of dining has been curtailed through grazing, snacking, and grabbing a bite to eat—forms of mere food consumption. The food itself has been reduced from a contextually intelligible and illuminating thing to an opaque if glamorous commodity.

Or consider the culture of the word, the traditional medium of world appropriation. People used to orient themselves in their world through the practice of writing letters, telling stories, engaging in conversations, attending plays, and reading to one another and through the silent reading of books and newspapers. Much of the practice that used to animate and sustain the culture of the word is captured in the term *literacy*. The things that used to center these practices do not have the tangibility of instruments and foods. But they were things just the same, commanding and illuminating realities, tales, plays, and texts.

31

Telephone and television are the technological devices that have weakened literacy and impoverished the culture of the word. Electronic machines have disburdened us of the demands of reading and writing. Once we had to impart our worlds through the work of writing or telling, and we had to gather our worlds laboriously from the promptings of writing and our fund of experiences and recollections. Now information is handed to us as readily available sounds and sights. Engagement with the world has been yielding to the consumption of news and entertainment commodities.

If we move outside the home to consider the balance of things and devices and of practices and consumption in the public realm, we come to see not only that things have yielded to devices as they have in the home, but also that the machinery side of public devices is much more prominent than their commodity side. Consider the two most imposing public devices that the second half of the last century has produced, the highway system and high-rise buildings. They serve the productive and administrative machinery by providing for trucking, accounting, or lawyering. Or they serve private rather than public consumption as they do in furnishing personal transportation or housing. Settings for public consumption are relatively rare though they are prominent enough. Examples are Disneyland and Disney World, theme parks, and shopping malls.

The prevalence of the instrumental side in the public realm is mirrored in the activity that is typically devoted to it, namely, labor. We pay for the liberty and prosperity of (largely private) consumption through labor, the construction and maintenance of the technological machinery, and labor is done almost entirely in the public realm if largely in its private sector.

Assessing the moral significance of the material culture, then, comes in large part to asking what the moral consequences of the rule of the device paradigm are. Here again we can depart from the findings of Csikszentmihalyi and Rochberg-Halton's investigation of the attitudes and reactions that correspond to stereos and musical instruments. Music plays a stronger role among children and adolescents than among adults, but quite generally stereos are used by people individually "as a modulator of emotions, a way of compensating for negative feelings."[21] A musical instrument, to the contrary, condenses "a whole complex set of meanings." Consider Csikszentmihalyi and Rochberg-Halton's account of a baritone ukulele's significance in a man's life.

> It allows the man to use his skills in musical expressions, to have fun in the present while reliving past enjoyment, and at the same time, sharing

the fun with those he loves. The ukulele in this case is a catalyst for a many-sided experience; it is not only an instrument for making sounds but is also a tool for a variety of pleasurable emotions. In playing it this man recaptures the past and binds his consciousness to that of others around him.[22]

Stereos appear to disengage people from their physical and social environment. When household objects are ranked according to the percentage of their meanings that respondents say refer to oneself, stereos rank second after television among eleven kinds of objects. Musical instruments rank fourth. When reference to others is the criterion, instruments rank fifth and stereos eighth.[23]

Considering other objects and criteria in Csikszentmihalyi and Rochberg-Halton's table, one finds, not surprisingly, that television, the only other technological device on the list, ranks even higher than stereos as a self-oriented object and as low as stereos in other-orientation. It is equally unsurprising if even more distressing that television and stereos rank first and second when it comes to meanings referring to experience (instruments ranking fourth). They rank last and third to last when reference is to memories (instruments rank seventh). One would also expect, as it turns out, that books, culturally most like instruments, rank very closely with the latter except in reference to others where books naturally rank much lower.[24]

Such objective data provide abstract lineaments that need to be given color and concrete detail as well as a broader interpretation. Csikszentmihalyi and Rochberg-Halton provide the latter through a concentric conception of the self. The narrowest sphere is the individual and personal, inevitably embedded in a wider social sphere, and in need of an inclusive, cosmic orientation.[25] Every traditional culture shows some such structure. But Csikszentmihalyi and Rochberg-Halton were surprised to find at most "a glimmer of the cosmic self" in the ways people talked about their homes.[26] The balance of the personal and the cosmic self seems very much upset in favor of the personal.[27]

In sum, material culture in the advanced industrial democracies spans a spectrum from commanding to disposable reality. The former reality calls forth a life of engagement that is oriented within the physical and social world. The latter induces a life of distraction that is isolated from the environment and from other people. There are pairs of terms that detail further the styles of life corresponding to the end points of the cultural continuum, namely, excellent vs. banal, deep vs. shallow, communal vs. individualist, celebratory vs. consumerist, and others.

This vocabulary appears ambiguous or peremptory without its proper complement of material culture. Ethics, to be truly illuminating, must become real. Theoretical and practical ethics, when abstracted from reality, become and remain partial, i.e., both limited and unwittingly tendentious. Taking liberal democratic ethics as an example of theoretical ethics, we can see that its devotion to equality is in danger of being trivialized and subverted as long as what is finally to be distributed in equal shares remains debilitatingly banal. And its devotion to equality is becoming increasingly shrill and ineffective because liberal theorists overlook the narcotic effect that disposable reality has on people.

If we let virtue ethics with its various traditional and feminist variants stand in for practical ethics, we must recognize that virtue, thought of as a kind of skilled practice, cannot be neutral regarding its real setting. Just as the skill of reading animal tracks will not flourish in a metropolitan setting, so calls for the virtues of courage and care will remain inconsequential in a material culture designed to procure a comfortable and individualist life.

What would be the major consequence of complementing theoretical and practical ethics with real ethics? It would be the realization that we make our crucial decisions not as individuals, as consumers, taxpayers, and voters who navigate their course in preestablished and rigid channels, but as citizens, and not just as citizens who pass on matters of civil rights and social welfare, but as citizens who take responsibility for the large design of our culture.

We do this most importantly not as consumers, taxpayers, or even voters, but as members of a community, and not as members of a community that serves some purpose beyond itself as does the PTA or the League of Women Voters. Such associations are certainly beneficial and commendable. But the most important communities are those that allow us as members to rest the case of what our lives are all about. They are communities of celebration.

3

Communities of Celebration

We live in a period of indecision and searching. In politics, the liberals had to yield their dominant position to the conservatives, but the latter have been unable to enact a distinctive and coherent program. In the arts, the relentlessly innovative vigor of modernism is spent, yet postmodernism has failed to do more than readmit superficially traditional elements. In social theory, the promise of rigorous analysis and effective solutions has faded. There has been a welcome dissolution of sterile disciplinary divisions and pretensions, but the newly fertile climate has yet to produce a vision of the common order that would inspire widespread and enduring enthusiasm. The only social force of undiminished vigor and self-confidence is technology. Sustained by scientific advances and fueled by magic prospects in electronics and genetics, technology continues to hold out the promise of millennial liberty and prosperity.

If we are ready to grant social theory the privilege of being society's bellwether, we can perhaps discern a new and hopeful movement. It springs from the endeavor to join the liberals' inclusive sense of social responsibility with the conservatives' regard for moral excellence and rootedness, and to do so in a forward-looking way. The old vocable "communitarianism" has been most widely used to name this new endeavor, and it is most often associated with the work of Robert Bellah, Alasdair MacIntyre, Michael Sandel, and Michael Walzer.

This possibility of a radical transformation of the common order may be remote, but the urgency for a communitarian turn of events is strong. At any rate, I accept the need for such a turn wholeheartedly. At the same time, I fear that the new movement got arrested by a combination of wistfulness and terror. Few people altogether reject the communitarian ideals, the spirit of selflessness, the sense of belonging, and the warmth of cooperation; but many believe that these ideals are either irretrievable or inseparable from pernicious complements, from paternalistic moralizing, suffocating provincialism, and totalitarian oppression. Terrified by these apprehensions, the critics of communitarianism have been stressing the virtues of the present liberal order; they have attacked the vagueness of their opponents and challenged them to demonstrate that communitarianism can be both carefully articulated and benign.[1] No one so far has risen to this challenge.

What has been left out in this debate and needs to be introduced is a consideration of the dailiness of life. But have not the liberal critics already called for concreteness and specificity on the part of the communitarians? And are not the liberals able to point to a well-articulated, if imperfectly realized, conception of the common order? They have and they are, but it is the genius of the present order that it conceals for its part the sort of moral issue that the communitarians are forced to confront as soon as they begin to work out their conception of the common order concretely. Hence, communitarianism seems to be burdened with a profoundly troubling problem of which liberalism appears to be entirely free. This is semblance only, however, and as long as it remains unchallenged, the common order of daily life will seem easily superior to communitarianism and remain dominant by default.

What really matters, of course, is not which of two schools of social theory will win, but that the concealment of the moral order is debilitating and needs to be lifted. Only after that has been done will communitarianism have the openness and space to propose a persuasive alternative. Communitarianism cannot be constructive without being critical. Accordingly, this chapter has two major parts. In the first I attempt to uncover the morally charged character of our concrete common order. I begin with a familiar aspect of the latter, namely, the public-private distinction, and try to show that it overlies a deeper and more consequential form of life, one whose vigor is rarely challenged or exposed—technology.

I concentrate my moral assessment of technology on the issue of public life and celebration and use celebration as an example to illustrate the moral liabilities of the technological way of life. Celebration is a helpful topic because celebration, if anything, constitutes the concrete and hopeful center of communal life. To clarify the difference between the technological and the communal versions of public celebration is to join the critical and the constructive tasks before us.

The second part of this chapter, then, is devoted to a description of communal celebration, of the celebrations that already exist in tentative and marginal ways, and of the measures we must take to give them a vigorous and central position in public life. It is not enough, however, to clear a space for communal celebration through criticism and then to fill it with reminders and suggestions of practices of celebration. Such proposals will seem so foreign to the body politic as presently constituted that they will be greeted, even by sympathetic readers, as transplants likely to be rejected. In a third part, therefore, I show that communities and practices of celebration, properly understood and supported, should be agreeable with the liberals' deeper and genuine concerns.

The possibilities of celebration in an advanced industrial society are delimited by technology. The shape that technology assumes in this case is the public-private distinction. This distinction exists in two dominant versions. Both have become so entrenched that they seem second nature to us. Accordingly, it seems obvious to us that the form of public celebration, favored by the public-private distinctions, is natural and legitimate and all other forms are not.

The philosophical task, therefore, is to expose the peculiarity of the prevailing public-private distinctions and to show that they are inimical to a vigorous public life. All this becomes visible when we learn to recognize that the public-private distinctions are characteristic concealments of technology, the latter taken as our distinctive form of life. Further, we must show just how technology through the public-private distinctions transforms and really eviscerates public celebration.

The two public-private distinctions are the economic and the social. The latter has the more direct ancestry in the depth of human history, and its power and peculiarity come into relief when seen as they emerge from the premodern period. In a broad sense, the public-private distinction is nearly as universal as human culture. This is so because something like the family is found in most cultures, and the family normally constitutes a relatively closed and intimate (i.e., private) environment, set off in some way from the common or public order that embraces all members of a village, tribe, or people.[2] In the common recollection of

European culture, the typical ferial setting of public life is the village community.[3] The prominent festal settings of our premodern European past were dominated by the church and nobility.[4] Our public aspirations are haunted to this day by the surveyable and personal life in the village community, and by the focused and festive splendor of religious and feudal celebrations. We have, of course, similar remembrances of Athens and of the early Roman republic.

At no point did public life of medieval character cease abruptly and entirely. Strands of it have survived to the present. But it did unravel gradually in the fire of the cultural and political conflagrations of the early modern period. Capitalism began to destroy the substance of the village community, and secularism began to supersede the cultural authority of religion and the feudal order. A distinctly modern successor arose in the London and Paris of the eighteenth century. The chief actor of this new public life was the newly prosperous and confident bourgeoisie. For a while, there was an artful celebration of public life, marked by stylized dress and speech, enacted in parks and streets, in theaters and coffeehouses.[5] For this achievement, the bourgeoisie borrowed heavily from the cultural treasures of the ancien régime. The challenge never met was the construction of a vigorous public life that would be both democratic and modern.

In the nineteenth century, the decay of public life began. It was a subtle sort of atrophy that was initially accompanied by an outward expansion of public facilities. This was the time when railway stations, department stores, libraries, and opera houses were erected as magnificent settings for the public to gather and enjoy itself. But the people who filled these spaces had become silent, passive, and distracted. No longer actors and connoisseurs of public spectacles, they had begun to turn into recipients and consumers of commodities, produced for them by experts.[6]

This largely negative picture of the fate of public life fails to disclose the reasons why these developments were so generally thought to be attractive and beneficial. There were two principal reasons: First, the apparent impoverishment of public culture was more than counterbalanced by a general sentiment of growing affluence. The nineteenth century was after all the time when the Industrial Revolution was beginning to make good the promise of prosperity that had inaugurated the modern era. More important, however, industrialization seductively specified the modern notion of prosperity that had been vague and implicit at first. It was prosperity based on the power of scientific insight and yielding freedom from the duress of nature and the demands of culture.[7]

I agree with Richard Sennett that public culture declined in the nineteenth and twentieth centuries. Still, a trenchant view of this development must include the gains that were taken to outweigh the losses. Fixed prices in the new department stores rendered transactions impersonal, but they also relieved the buyer of having to challenge the seller. Advertising, to be sure, was often fanciful to the point of fraudulence, but it did heighten and sanction the customers' acquisitive desires.[8] Paganini's and Liszt's pyrotechnics tended to reduce compositions to a mere means, but they disburdened the listeners from having to know or judge the merits of a composition as well. And the silence of the newly passive audience liberated one from the irritations and impositions of rude or vociferous listeners.[9]

The other reason for the attractiveness of the nineteenth-century developments that must be kept in view is this: The leisure side of public life was declining, to be sure. But the labor side was growing enormously and diverted attention from the loss of public leisure. As labor moved out of the family, it became a public affair, something that was done out in the open, requiring cooperation with strangers and conformity with impersonal rules. These changes in the habits of work went hand in hand with the rise of imposing public structures: bridges, roads, harbors, mines, factories, and many more. Many of these public structures belong, of course, to the private sector. This inconsistency of usage concerns us below.

In the twentieth century, a yet more radical transformation of the public realm took place. The most obvious and typical manifestation was the construction of highways and high-rises. The highways reshaped space in its horizontal dimension, the skyscrapers in the vertical dimension. In all of human history there has never been so massive a reordering of public space. Remarkably, both of these new kinds of public structure have an avowedly subservient or instrumental position in our culture; they are means to an end. Expressways are meant to get the commuter from home to work and goods from one place to another. High-rise buildings for the most part contain offices where people do work that is not usually considered ennobling or rewarding apart from the money to which it is a means.

Naturally, we feel a desire to center our culture in its most prominent tangible expressions. We are moved to celebrate the highways as the distinctive way in which we appropriate this country and to see in the

39

skyline of a metropolis the embodiment of modern power and sophistication. But these sentiments are belied by the grim or sullen moods that we exhibit when we drive on the expressways or work in our offices.

Thus, the public sphere of the twentieth century has become both hypertrophied and atrophied, both excessively developed in its sheer physical presence and devoid of intrinsic or final dignity, bereft of celebration and festivity.[10] This unhappy condition of the public sphere is aggravated by the absence of a counterbalancing sphere of finality or celebration. As public space has been taken over by instrumentality (i.e., production and administration), finality (i.e., consumption) has passed into the private realm. The latter must remain inconspicuous because of the nature of privacy.

Privacy, unlike the private realm, is a uniquely contemporary social phenomenon and is best understood when seen in its legal setting. We think of privacy today as both eminently desirable and frequently threatened. This tension has naturally led to litigation and to the United States Supreme Court; but privacy has no explicit mention in the Constitution. Hence, to protect privacy, the court had to search the penumbra of the Bill of Rights for grounds to do so.[11]

There is not only a problem of saying why privacy should be protected, there is the prior difficulty of saying what privacy is and what constitutes a violation of it. Privacy is something different from autonomy or personal liberty, for it is possible to grant someone freedom in all personal regards, and still to invade his or her privacy through snooping or eavesdropping. Nor is just any intrusion of the personal realm a violation of privacy. Some, such as unwanted noises or odors, are merely nuisances.[12]

Reasoning along these lines, Thomas Huff has helpfully isolated the notion of privacy as freedom from intrusions that can lead to an unwarranted judgment on the person whose sphere of intimacy has been invaded. Of course, our next of kin, who are naturally members of our personal circle, and our friends, whom we have invited into it, are entitled to judge whatever we do. No one else may without our permission.[13]

Such a notion of privacy would have remained sharply limited and largely uninteresting in a pretechnological, i.e., premodern setting, where the highly contextual nature of work and celebration was mirrored in a greater continuity of family and community. Families identified themselves with and through the moral standards and judgments of the community, and they depended on communal cooperation for entertainment and celebration. With the rise and progressive articulation of modern prosperity and liberty, these communal ties came to be seen as burdens. Consumption is the imperious and unencumbered enjoyment of goods or commodities. What Huff calls the privacy norm is in large part the collective affirmation of consumption as an exercise of freedom that would be encumbered by judgmental intrusion. Intrusion by whom? Huff speaks of the private realm as "that part of our lives conducted with families and friends."[14] But we increasingly withdraw from the judgments of our friends, parents, and spouses, too. Ultimately, the realm of privacy is in each case occupied by one consumer.

If consumption is located in millions of separate compartments, finality and celebration are accordingly scattered and inconspicuous. It is possible, of course, to aggregate a thousand condominiums into a soaring and gleaming tower, but such a structure no more bespeaks a spirit of festive engagement and public celebration than does an office highrise building from which it is outwardly indistinguishable.

Consideration of the social public-private distinction reveals the emergence of a division between public machineries of production and administration and a realm of private compartments for the consumption of commodities. Revealed in this division is the pattern of modern technology, the shape on which the application of science, the ingenuity of engineering, and the energy of industry have been converging. The emergence of this pattern is not caused by scientific necessity, by engineering convictions, or by industrial aspirations. It is simply the configuration that the several parts of modern culture are assuming. Technology, as I have argued, is a helpful vocable for this emergent structure, although surely not the only possible one.

In spite of the entrenchment and power of technology, we are reluctant to recognize it, and inclined to confuse and conceal our implication in it. The significance of the economic public-private distinction is that it provides us with an arrangement and a rhetoric that enable us to avoid explicit responsibility for the common order and to ignore the impoverishment of public life. To show how responsibility and impoverishment are intertwined and jointly concealed, I discuss side by side, more or less, the economic public-private distinction and two affairs that were as public and celebratory as technology would permit.

The economic distinction between the public and private gets its semantic flavor from the noun it qualifies, namely, "sector." Talk of the public and private sectors is common in political and economic discourse, and at first it seems as though this distinction had nothing in common with the social distinction just considered. It is obvious that the two distinctions are not parallel.[15] Both the private and the public sectors fall within the public realm in the social sense. Both are sectors of the public machinery of production and administration. Both are distinct from the areas of leisure, consumption, and strictly personal discretion.

To see how the economic public-private distinction hides our implication in the common order, let us begin by defining the public sector in the conventional way. It is thought to consist of three parts. First, there is the government with its machinery, the bureaucracy, and the personnel that immediately serve the three branches of government as they design and enact public policy. Second, there are certain means of producing goods and services that belong to the state, such as timber and grazing lands, the educational system, the National Weather Service, and so on. Finally, there is the share of the total social resources that is collected and spent by the government for the public good through private enterprise, e.g., the tax funds given to private construction firms to build or maintain highways, to produce weapons, or to reforest public lands. The rest of the economy constitutes the private sector.

In party politics the distinction between the private and the public sector looms large. Conservatives generally favor the first and liberals the second. From the standpoint of what social structure and its technological pattern require, the economic distinction is superficial and misleading, but it helps us to cope with our unsettled attitudes toward the technological society.[16] To see this, consider the organization of the 1984 Olympics and the restoration of the Statue of Liberty. These were clearly public tasks and, under a liberal administration, would have been supported with public revenue. Instead, they were turned over to inspired leaders from the private sector, Peter Ueberroth and Lee Iacocca, who raised hundreds of millions of dollars from private corporations.

Conservatives find this approach appealing because it promises to avoid the coercive and inefficient hand of the government, and to engage instead the initiative and self-reliance of the individual. Closer inspection of these two enterprises shows, however, that they were more public than private, not only in the social but in the economic sense as well. The government had in effect given Ueberroth and Iacocca a well-defined taxing authority by entrusting them exclusively with a prominent national task, and with the use of valued symbols. Both Ueberroth and Iacocca were quick to invoke the force of the law when they saw encroachments on their exclusive authority. Given such power, it was relatively easy to force the hand of large corporate givers who came forward with gifts of several million dollars at a stroke. The government supported these supposedly private enterprises in other ways as well. It put the U.S. Treasury and U.S. Mint at their disposal to raise tens of millions, and it contributed, in effect, the tax revenue, again in the tens of millions, that was lost because the corporate gifts were tax-deductible.

Even the large remainder of funds that in one sense came undeniably from economically private sources did not do so in another. The corporations did not collect their millions through contributions from their members. The corporate gifts did not represent sacrifices as one would expect of private contributions. Rather, the money came from advertising budgets that in turn are supported from earnings which, finally, come from the consumers. In effect, every buyer of MacDonald's hamburgers or Kodak film was assessed a few cents to support the Olympics or the Statue of Liberty, and in this sense the consumer came to be a taxpayer. To be sure, not everyone did pay up unwillingly; but many, certainly, did so unknowingly. Even then, the assessments were not coercive, but the cost in time and energy of avoiding corporate sponsors would have exceeded the benefit, if any, of avoiding the assessments.[17]

These are particularly clear examples of how socially public celebrations, supposedly based on economically private endeavors, are enmeshed with the public sector. There are equally clear examples of public-spirited endeavors that hardly at all rely on the government or on assessments to the consumer-taxpayer, e.g., cases where people in a local setting collect money from individual persons to support a charity or a sport. There is a continuum between the truly and the nominally private institutions that promote public causes, a continuum on which at various places one would locate the United Way, symphony societies, private universities, and many other institutions.

All of these examples merely illustrate a broader thesis, put forward by John Kenneth Galbraith in 1967, to the effect that, in the new industrial state, government, business, the unions, and the educational and scientific estates form but one coherent system beyond the public-private distinction.[18] This, of course, is not to say that the new industrial system fails to have functionally distinct parts or that it is unimportant to keep those parts distinct. It is just to point out that from the economic and technological point of view, the economic public-private distinction draws a peculiarly confusing line of distinction.

But there is method to our confusion. It allows us to avoid the burden of explicit responsibility for the decisive cast of our lives, namely, technology. One can only avoid, however, what in some sense one recognizes. The character of technology, at a deep and implicit level, is well understood by the citizens of this country.[19] There is a common and tacit agreement to shape the world and conduct one's life according to the technological pattern. This agreement has given our society its stability and resilience, and since we are basically in agreement, we have the license of denying our misgivings and discontents about the common order at the surface of politics.

Thus, entrusting public celebrations to the private sector allows us to pretend that we do not have to pay for them. When *Time* and *Newsweek* as much as tell us that we have to after all, we are not disturbed. We knew all along, at least at the deeper and more implicit level, that nothing comes from nothing. What is troubling, however, to anyone who values the dignity of politics is the ease and radicality with which people have surrendered the determination of public life to the machinery of technology. People appear to have no desire to claim, through their elected representatives, the authority and responsibility for the staging of public celebrations.

This of course leads us to the point, reached above from another angle, that in any substantive sense there is hardly a public life anymore. Politics has become technology of last resort, the governor that regulates the machinery of production and administration. Far from desiring or enjoying government, people seem to be annoyed by it. They want to be disburdened of it and are reluctant to support it directly and consciously through taxes, but again their resentment does not threaten or revoke their basic acceptance of technology. In some way, so they realize, the machinery of society must be supported. Thus, while the federal tax reform of 1986 lightened the tax burden for most individuals, it increased corporate taxes. And the latter make their way to the individual via higher prices just the same. This is rarely emphasized in the political debates, but neither is it a closely guarded secret. It is enveloped by the same twilight that shrouds people's pact with technology.

Although the technological society is stable and resilient, it is shallow, too, having lost dimensions of life that we used to value. The loss of vigorous politics, i.e., the loss of an active, shared, and ennobling determination of the common order, is a diminishment of public life. An analogous loss is visible not just in the organization but also in the quality of the public celebrations that we have been considering. Two matters that at the time received wide publicity shed light on this privation: the commercialization of these events, and the important role

44

of David Wolper.[20] What we see here is an extension and aggravation of the malady that Sennett first found in the nineteenth century.

Commercialization, as Fred Hirsch has pointed out, is the conversion of a genuinely common or public good into one that can be bought by the individual and privately consumed.[21] Even when people are out in the open and in the public realm, one prominent way in which they celebrate a public event is to buy something that they can possess individually and take home.

We must also remember that, if thousands witnessed the Olympic games in the stadium, millions did so through television in the privacy of their homes. And as we all know, the television picture is more sophisticated, more embroidered and privileged than any that can be had from the grandstand, which brings us to the role that David Wolper played at these two celebrations.[22] He was the impresario who fabricated the crowning events at the Olympics and the celebration of the Statue of Liberty. In his hands, the common and cultural achievements of this country became raw material that Wolper molded and arranged for the greatest possible impact on the viewers. People no longer had to work to gather and grasp the meaning of the many things they witnessed. Wolper at once disburdened and overwhelmed them.

Here again I have concentrated on the tendency of technology to dissolve the depth of a genuinely public and celebratory life into a sophisticated machinery that yields an easily and safely consumable commodity.[23] To be sure, in the interstices of machinery and commodity, groups of people did celebrate publicly and vigorously.[24] And, moving now to a more general level, the economic public-private distinction not only serves to conceal our implication in technology and to express our discontents with this arrangement, it also bespeaks, in a frustrated way, people's desire for a kind of moral excellence and sanction that the technological system in its undisguised form cannot provide.

The conservatives, particularly, continue to feel the appeal of the traditional virtues, and they desire to hold their privileges with the sanction of traditional morality. The notion of the private provides it admirably. It draws from the concept of the private in the social sense the force of personal freedom and initiative, and so engenders the illusion that whatever is part of the private sector has been earned in free competition and merited by personal initiative.

The conservative attitude is not the idiosyncrasy of an elite but reflects a widely shared, if usually unrealized and universally unrealizable, aspiration. The liberals mistakenly believe that people largely

45

desire an equal distribution of affluence. It appears, however, that above a floor of universally assured welfare, people find the blessings of technology most alluring in an arrangement of inequality. Most people look upon the favored position of the conservatives not with reproach, but with envy. And as long as a minimum standard of living is assured for all, most people would rather aspire to a privileged position of luxury than actually share a lesser position with everyone else.[25] Like the conservatives, we would like our privileges to be the manifestation of moral excellence, and so we lend a willing ear to the conservative rhetoric of traditional values.

To sum up, if we are concerned to promote a more communal common order and if we agree that public celebration is at the heart of community, then we must recognize and take issue with modern technology and the public-private distinctions that both articulate and conceal it. The social distinction makes genuine public celebration impossible because the public realm is for production, not celebration, and though the private realm is for leisure, leisure is now commodious consumption, not festive engagement. And if it were the latter, it would still be subject to the confinement of privacy.

The economic distinction allows us to act as though we could avoid responsibility for this impoverishment of our common life. The public sector is the realm of explicitly responsible citizenship, but we are reluctant to embrace it as the forum to shape and support the common order or as the place for common celebrations. Instead, we shift these tasks in large part to the private sector. This works well enough since technology undergirds and interconnects the two sectors, and it does so with our implicit approval. The price of our indirection is the evisceration of politics and the replacement of genuine celebration with the counterfeit of spectacles produced for consumption.

From the consideration of the social distinction between the public and private realms we should draw the lesson that we must challenge modern technology if we are to make room for communal celebration. The examination of the economic distinction should teach us that we are implicated in the determination of the common order, like it or not, and that we had better assume our responsibility openly and constructively. This entails particularly that we should permit ourselves neither to be frightened by, nor to seek cover behind, the current definition of the public and the private sectors. Such frankness, moreover, will prevent our traditional moral aspirations from being deflected into private and acquisitive diffidence.

46

How then can we hope to give communities of celebration a central place in a technological society? Community, to begin with, is generally used to designate a number of people with a common bond of some sort, a common interest or habit. In this sense, the gun owners, the joggers, or the viewers of a television program form a community.[26] I want to use community in a stronger sense, one that is close to Robert Bellah's notion of a community of memory and of practices of commitment, and refers to a group of people who are in one another's bodily presence and engaged in a common enterprise that is an end rather than a means.[27]

Although stronger, this notion of community is weaker than the one used by sociologists in distinction from that of a society. I referred to this concept above to characterize the prevailing common order prior to the rise of modern technology. A community in this sense shares not just one thing but nearly everything, not just celebration but also work, residence, religion, and ancestry. Communities in this sense are rare and precarious today; for good reason, their establishment and promotion in this country must be rejected as the goal of public policy.

Turning to celebration, we can think of it broadly as the public performance of a solemn or entertaining enterprise. In this case we can come closer to the sense that concerns me by distinguishing it from three that anthropologists have explicated. The first two are correlative, play and ritual. Play is a celebration that mimics, mocks, and criticizes the prevailing power relations in a society. Ritual is a celebration that sanctions and solemnizes an existing social establishment.[28] Third, one might think of celebration as a text that, properly interpreted, tells us how a community interprets itself.[29]

I do not deny that celebrations may have these functions, but what a technological society needs are celebrations in a different, namely, real and focal sense. The three anthropological senses of celebration dematerialize the things that are at their center. Those things do not really matter. Thus, Clifford Geertz says of the Balinese cockfight: "For it is only apparently that cocks are fighting there. Actually it is men."[30] I am in no position to dispute this view of the Balinese case, but I want to point out that the dematerialization of central things is congenial to technology; a celebration wherein concrete things are really secondary is susceptible to technological subversion. If it is men who actually fight and not cocks, could not the men use video games, financial instruments, or cars as proxies? In a certain sense they could, of course, but under the aegis of that sense, the difference between a premodern and

47

a technological society evaporates, and, most important, the peculiar liabilities of the latter remain concealed.

A celebration, then, in the sense that I want to use here, is centered on some concrete thing. It is a joyful engagement with the physical presence and radiance of that thing. The latter, within narrow limits, is central and indispensable to the celebration. In calling this the real and focal sense of celebration, I want to draw on the old meaning of "real," namely, thing-like, and on the centering and radiating force that is conveyed by "focal."

In some instances, the physical reality required by a community of celebration can be austere indeed. Gymnastics requires only a level, hard, and springy floor. Folk or square dancing in addition needs a fiddle or piano. But space, reduced to utter simplicity, rarely comes to life as vividly as it does in tumbling or dancing. It is seldom as spacious and rich as when it is so artfully filled and appropriated by humans.

When we think of a gymnastics club housed in an abandoned warehouse, or of square dancing taking place in the basement of a housing project, we are alerted to the connection between the real and the focal aspects of a celebration. Although in the cases just suggested, tumbling and dancing have the minimal space they need, the indifference or hostility of the wider physical context in effect dampens and denies the festivity and radiance of these practices. Communal celebrations will be salutary and central for our lives only if the material things and settings that ground and nourish them are granted public and prominent locations.

We must next try to gain a tentative overview of what kinds of communal celebration are actual and possible today. To obtain that survey, we should turn to the typical setting of contemporary life and cast our net wide. The typical setting is the megalopolis. It is of course an urban setting, but it is typical in a way that transcends the traditional contrast of urban and rural, as Lawrence Haworth has pointed out:

> City and country once signified two distinct styles of life, and the nation was two nations side by side. This is no longer true: the two styles are coalescing into one, in the same way that all classes are moving into the middle class. The truer image is that of a nation becoming urban, not merely in the sense that cities are growing outward, but in the deeper social sense that styles of life are becoming uniform, and uniformly urban. Megalopolis is a vanguard.[31]

Clearly, if we are unable to find or imagine communities of celebration in a megalopolitan setting, the prospects of a vigorous contemporary public life are doomed, but we should not settle for just any sort of communal celebration. They must be possible in the open, generally accessible spaces of the megalopolis; they must be public.

We should take a wide and generous view of communal celebrations to practice the kind of sensitivity and receptivity needed to recognize and advance genuine reform. At the same time, we must avoid aimlessness. I suggest we center our view on clear and eminent cases where a community is actively engaged in a celebration, and centered on a definite public thing.

A softball league, playing throughout the summer in a city park, is a case in point. The participants are players, not spectators. They delight in their skills and teamwork. It is the open and verdant center of the city that they appropriate in their playing. It is the easy living of summer that they enjoy. We may abbreviate the human excellence of the communal celebration in calling it active; we can capture the celebrants' intimacy with a great and prominent thing in calling the celebration focused. Active and focused communities of celebration shade over into more passive and diffuse ones. People who go to a concert attend a focused celebration but do so more passively. People who enjoy walking or running through a city are actively engaged; but their engagement has a more diffuse setting.

It is helpful to mark off the boundaries of communal celebration by considering the limits of diffusion and passivity. The extreme and degenerate case of a diffuse public setting is indifference. A physical setting is indifferent when location and integration in the larger environment are accidental or contingent on efficiency. Shopping centers and malls are indifferent in this sense. Their indifference often clashes with the designers' attempts to give malls and shopping centers a striking spatial or historical appearance, but this overlay of culture is immaterial. One can readily imagine the mall's disappearance and its replacement by computerized video shopping from the comfort of one's home. It must be this dissonance between spatial pretensions and functional indifference that induces mall nausea.

Passivity of communal celebration has its limit and decay in disengagement, the human counterpart to environmental indifference. Shoppers are disengaged from the fullness of their capacities and their environment. The same is true of drivers who in a superficial sense are active and form a community, but who fail to be deeply in touch with their surroundings.

49

Indifference and disengagement are the ways in which technology has invaded and subverted public life and left us with a semblance of the public. For that reason, active and focused celebrations constitute the powerful and hopeful center for a public renewal. This point is overlooked by social philosophers who take the ideal, if vaguely conceived, setting for public life to be an open space that accommodates a rich mixture of institutions and activities.[32]

Michael Walzer calls such public spaces open-minded to distinguish them from the single-minded spaces that are devoted to just one purpose.[33] To be sure, the latter term captures indifferent and disengaging technological structures such as shopping centers and highways. But as Michael Rustin has replied, bird sanctuaries, music festivals, and yachting marinas are single-minded institutions and yet conducive to communal celebration.[34] Conversely, as Marshall Berman points out, Disney Worlds–by-the-sea can be open-minded in Walzer's sense and yet "absent-minded," i.e., indifferent in their larger setting and distracting to their visitors.[35]

Berman himself, however, is not sufficiently attentive to the power and depth of focused engagement in public life. What he admires and would like to promote in public spaces is a kind of free-floating theatricality that is reminiscent of the bourgeois public life, extolled by Sennett.[36] Surely, we should welcome and encourage this sort of public celebration, particularly because it provides an opening for the kind of spontaneous cultural growth we must nurture and cherish. At the same time, we should look closely and in a more focused way at present communal celebrations where people do not just play at something, but in playing are definite persons, where they do not just take up some role on some stage, but are fully engaged in this, their own place, and where they do not just send and receive messages in some fashionable code, but encounter one another in the depths of their being.

This brings me to the explanation of communities of celebration where I invite the reader to look at particular cases. Everything and nothing depends on the following illustrations. Everything depends on their reality and intrinsic vigor, but nothing depends on any one of these instances. The public support of communities of celebration is essentially a pluralist affair. If other and brighter instances come to the reader's mind, so much the better.

Let me begin with street-corner music and illustrate, first of all, the point that communal celebrations will not arise from abstract designs. Modern classical music has suffered from an excess of abstract design and has therefore, in spite of substantial institutional support, failed to inspire popular communities of celebration. Street-corner music, on the other hand, in all its classical, jazz, and popular varieties, has sprung up and spontaneously attracted communities of listeners.

Granted, only the musicians constitute a community in the active and focused sense. The audience is usually anonymous, sporadic, and passive. But a community is not an all-or-nothing affair. The bodily presence, the skill, the engagement, and the goodwill of the musicians radiate into the listeners and transform them to some degree. It becomes obvious here that theatricality is not enough. The performers cannot just pretend to be musicians. Struggling amateurs will not for long be able to engage their listeners. The musicians must be competent in their own right.

Another way of highlighting the significance of engagement for the vigor of communal celebrations is to consider someone sitting at a street corner making music with a tape recorder. The music as mere sound may be greatly superior to what street musicians would accomplish, but the sound would not be rooted in the presence of things and persons, in instruments and performers here and now. The music would be shallow and at best would serve as a means of calling attention to a beggar.

Music as a celebration that is real all the way down will also sink its roots into the reality of the public space where it takes place. Celebration and place will inform one another. Thus, although street-corner music is not and should never be the result of a design thought up by public officials, surely much can and ought to be done to make the physical environment of the city more generous to such music. It is a matter of providing space, shelter, and a little quiet in the midst of the urban commotion, and comfortable seating for the audience. These settings should be sufficiently thoughtful and beautiful to express our admiration for the music and the musicians. There is also a need for coordination. Not all possible groups can be accommodated at the favorite places. There needs to be some selecting, spacing, and scheduling. Finally there has to be a more or less formal common understanding of the economic rights and obligations of the musicians and the listeners.

Surely these tasks can only be solved publicly, i.e., with the help of those persons who alone are empowered and enabled by all of us to act effectively. And surely how those tasks are solved will have a large bearing on just how prosperous, festive, and communal street-corner music will become. It is crucial to prevent public arrogance and design from overtaking the spontaneity of celebration. Public support must be extended in a spirit of service, experiment, and fairness. The musicians and their experiences must retain a guiding role, and whatever setting and organization street-corner music settles into with public help, these arrangements must remain open to further development.

Next, let me turn more directly to the issue of realism, i.e., to the importance of having a concrete thing as the focus of our celebration. More light falls on this point when we turn to the unlikely case of tennis. Clearly, the real side of tennis, the court, has in its normal contemporary version suffered impoverishment compared with the stately late medieval courts and the verdant lawns of English gardens. Such real richness cannot be recovered for today, but we can enhance the focal power of tennis courts by situating them out of doors in central and aesthetically favored locations, surrounded by facilities where people can sit, watch, talk, and refresh themselves. To be sure, in the heat of a match, the larger physical surrounding, no matter how magnificent, evaporates into an implicit and immaterial periphery. But there is more to tennis than the intensity of the game. It is being with friends, exposing our competence to public view, glorying in our skills, learning from our betters. It should also be a way in which we physically appropriate a central space in our city and bodily experience its moods in the passage of the seasons. Such appropriate inhabitation is in marked contrast to the fleeting and furtive ways in which we normally pass through our public spaces.

Here again it appears obvious to me that only society as a whole has the means and authority to establish and maintain such tennis courts. And here, too, the practitioners themselves, the tennis players, should have the lead in determining the layout of the courts, the assignment of playing time, the staging of tournaments, etc. Here, too, we can see how communal celebration and public space are reciprocal. Conventional tennis courts are single-minded in Walzer's sense, and therefore adequate for competition but adverse to celebration. If they are set in an environment favorable to walking about and sharing a drink, public space has become more open-minded.

I come to the most difficult and important case of communal celebrations, those of religious character. My point has been that public life requires communal celebrations, and that communities of celebration need public support. But since Jefferson there has been a strongly held position that church and state be separated by a wall. This position draws strength and legitimacy from an undeniable history of religious intolerance and persecution. I return to these concerns below. Here, I want to consider the reasons why we should publicly support religious communities of celebration, and then call attention to one that deserves such support.

There are formal and substantive considerations why a vigorous public life needs publicly supported religious celebrations. The formal ones come into view when we distinguish between engaging and reflective celebrations. This is a distinction of fact, not a disjunction of conceptual necessity. Let me explain. Tennis is an engaging celebration in that it calls forth our participation forcefully and in many ways. Tennis can draw us into the excitement of a game to the point where the wider context of time and place recedes into an indistinct and no longer noticed background. The game engages our speed, coordination, strength, cunning, gallantry, and cooperation; but tennis is not reflective. It does not explicitly gather in and reflect the larger and largest contexts of life. We now have several adjectives to name the various dimensions and frameworks of reality: traditional, cultural, political, ecological, and cosmological. All of them used to be simultaneously collected and reflected in religious celebrations.[37] These aspects and realms exist in a scattered way to this day. Clearly, public life is poorer the less these dimensions are united and reflected in one celebration.

Our national celebrations are attempts at reflective and festive gatherings, but they are often painfully flat and unengaging since by design and under the stern countenance of the First Amendment, as it were, they exclude what in fact provides the deepest reflective occasion for most citizens, that is, religious celebration. This is the substantive consideration in favor of public support for religious celebrations. It is simply the case that most people in this country find their deepest orientation in religion.[38] As members of the national community we ought to affirm this devotion explicitly. As long as we officially ignore it, our public life will remain empty.

The reflective power of religious celebration has astonishing appeal. No political or cultural institution draws people so regularly and in such great numbers out of their homes and into a community. Whatever charges one might bring against the national culture, it certainly does not pressure or seduce people into attending religious worship. The faithful today come from an authentic need.

It must be the need for reflective religious celebration since religious service has become rather unengaging. With few exceptions, most churches have failed for several generations now to inspire or incorporate great art.[39] Hence, one might say that the public needs religious communities of celebration; religion, in turn, needs the inspiration of real and focal celebration. I believe that the churches can hope again to become vital forces in our culture only if they learn to be genuine communities of celebration in the sense described above. That means that they have to give up on abstract designs handed down by a hierarchy. Instead, they must listen to the Holy Spirit that animates people in unforethinkable ways. Religion must also recover a sense of realism that asserts the sacramental dignity of things and practices against their conversions into commodities for consumption.

Openness to the Holy Spirit and a sense of sacramental realism are practiced, I believe, in the work and celebrations that are going on in the Cathedral of St. John the Divine in New York.[40] There is an ecumenical acceptance of Christian, Jewish, Islamic, and East Asian worship, a generous hospitality toward the arts and crafts, and a reaching out to the poor and the powerless. There is no problem of intolerance here. Atheists are welcome and feel at home in St. John's. St. John's is public in its generosity, and so deserves and would benefit from public support. I realize that strong liberal reservations remain. I answer these below. If those reservations can be met positively, then it will also have been shown that the communitarian aspirations can be worked out positively and concretely.

Let me now place the notion of communities of celebration in a wider scholarly context. To urge communities of celebration is to press for a reform of technology, the latter taken as the predominant way in which we take up with reality today. Technology, I said above, has a distinctive pattern whose prime feature is a division and correlation of means and ends, of machinery and commodity, production and consumption, labor and leisure, the public and the private. To urge the public affirmation of communities of celebration is to cut across the dominant divisions; it is to recommend the reinvigoration of public leisureliness.[41]

Such a recommendation must face up to the problem of tolerance and the politics of community. Liberals generally assume that a devotion to community inevitably leads to intolerance. But this follows only, as Christopher Lasch has noted, if we cling to an organic and sentimental notion of community. "Social solidarity," Lasch holds to the contrary, "does not rest on shared values or ideological consensus, let alone on an identity of interests; it rests on a public conversation."[42] With Michael Sandel, we can go further and argue that a public conversation, inspired by communitarian responsibility, is more likely to

54

assure tolerance than a liberal society of individuals who refuse to share and affirm their deepest convictions publicly. This is the force of Sandel's remarks that

> intolerance flourishes most where forms of life are dislocated, roots unsettled, traditions undone. In our day, the totalitarian impulse has sprung less from the convictions of confidently situated selves than from the confusions of atomized, dislocated, frustrated selves, at sea in a world where common meanings have lost their force.[43]

However tolerant one may agree to be in the communitarian spirit, does not the First Amendment strictly exclude religion as a positive concern of public conversation? To be sure, the amendment has almost universally come to be taken this way, but neither the wording nor the origin of the First Amendment prohibit more than the establishment of one national religion.[44] Granted that, the issue must be reopened in what Lasch calls

> a conversational relationship with the past, one that seeks neither to deny the past nor to achieve an imaginative restoration of the past but to enter into a dialogue with the traditions that still shape our view of the world, open in ways in which we are not even aware.[45]

The crucial point is to open and sustain this conversation. At length, I would hope, it will lead to the political affirmation of communities of celebration. But it would certainly violate the spirit of community if one would make public support of religion the sine qua non of one's commitment to public celebration.

Disagreement, then, is not just tolerable but natural in communal politics. It is crucial, however, to urge that the disagreements be substantial. Liberals tend to reduce the political agenda to the question of civic membership, spelled out in terms of rights.[46] This, they remind the communitarians, is the burning and unsolved problem, one that the communitarians, so the liberals continue, are more likely to aggravate then alleviate. Walzer has well shown, I believe, that the question of membership is primary and distinct in the pursuit of justice, but that it certainly does not exhaust the proper domain of politics.[47] In liberal theory the exclusive stress on rights and membership leads to a debilitating one-sidedness. It suppresses the question of what sort of common order it is that we want to give everyone admission to. Consequently, liberalism ends up protecting technology as a way of life from critical scrutiny. Nor

55

would criticism alone be sufficient. It tends to become aimless and dispiriting unless guided by a substantive concern. Communitarianism provides it generally, and communal celebration constitutes it concretely.

I am not disavowing the liberal concern for full or equal membership in the nation. I favor using the force of the law to support the poor and the powerless, women, homosexuals, racial minorities, the disabled, and alien residents. But the popular appeal of these measures has miserably flagged for over a generation now, so the substance of the common order should concern us not just in its own right, but as a way to equal membership in it as well.

Indeed, there is a principled tie between communal celebration and justice. To begin with a less than burning and yet deeply distressing issue of injustice that can only be solved through public support of celebration, consider Richard Sennett's remarks:

> It is estimated that there are eight hundred classical pianists in New York City trying to have full concert careers; there are five concert halls in the city which "count"; in a given year, from thirty to thirty-five of the eight hundred will appear solo in these halls. Of the thirty, at least half are so well known that they appear year after year. Around fifteen new pianists get a hearing in New York each year. . . . These new pianists get a paragraph in the *Times* which describes them as "promising" or "accomplished," and then they sink back into obscurity.[48]

Obviously, this system inflicts a terrible injustice on our best young musicians and on the vast American hinterland that has little resident excellence in music, no highly focused communities of musical celebration, no practices of commitment to art. As Sennett points out clearly, if implicitly, it is the force of technology that concentrates, or rather, constricts, the exercise of music to a few centers and at the same time procures performance as a commodity.[49] Only public conversation and action can remedy this prostitution and injustice.

The more urgent and pervasive aspect of the connection between justice and celebration comes to the fore when we remember that the rich can always buy memberships in communities of celebration, in country clubs, health spas, symphony societies, and, indirectly, in Lake Forest's Episcopalian parish. But as Robert Bellah and his coauthors have well pointed out, the reproach of exclusiveness and idleness rests on such "lifestyle enclaves."[50] Being exclusive, they are not deeply communal; being marginal to the public centers of power and excellence, they are not really celebratory.

It follows that communities of celebration deserve public support only if they have open membership, i.e., anyone must be able to join as long as he or she is devoted to the cause the community has been established to celebrate. Practical circumstances such as overcrowding may require modifications, but the principle of open membership must remain the norm.[51]

Open membership will also be conducive to the kind of interpersonal relationship needed to invigorate public life. We often and invidiously contrast communal warmth and intimacy with the cold anonymity of modern society. Richard Sennett has tried to expose intimacy as an altogether uncivilizing and enervating force, a pernicious and irredeemable tyranny.[52] I think this is an extreme and extravagant, though provocative, argument. Even those who favor intimacy in the family and oppose anonymity at large recognize that genuine public life requires a certain impersonality.[53] This seems an unfortunate term to me although I accept what it intends: a friendly openness on definite terms. Intimacy requires an unconditional closeness that becomes strained when extended to greater numbers of people, and fraudulent when offered to the public.[54] But how are we to define the terms of public openness and engagement?

One way, mentioned above, is theatricality, the spectacular enactment of conventions of dress, movement, and speech. Again, such public interaction should be welcomed. Still, communities of celebration, I believe, allow us to encounter one another on deeper and yet well-defined terms. In a tennis game, persons reveal their timidity or gallantry, their awkwardness or grace, their acrimony or good humor. They generally do so in a way that avoids the artless narcissism Sennett finds objectionable in intimacy.

To be sure, theatricality and celebratory self-disclosure are not disjoint. Conventions of politeness and courtesy help us to participate enjoyably in celebrations. At any rate, it appears that communities of celebration can sponsor a social condition that is well placed between the intimacy of the family and the anonymity of mass society. That condition and attitude is properly called community. The spirit of community fosters both the pleasure of acquaintance among people who regularly meet one another in celebration and the friendly openness that invites newcomers to join in.

I have pleaded for a realist view of celebrations. When the latter are centered on concrete things and practices, celebrants tend to be secure and serene in the devotion to their cause. Tennis players love their game.

They teach their children and invite their friends to play it, but they will not insist, nor will they crusade against musicians. In fact, they may be musicians also or have friends and relatives who are. Communities of celebration overlap and interconnect; we are apt to take pleasure in such diversity, and enjoy in the talents and practices of others what for one reason or another is denied to us.[55]

I do not want to belittle the need for continued vigilance against communal intolerance. Broadly based historical communities as well as contemporary communities centered on a narrow issue of self-interest have inflicted terrible misery on outsiders. It is surely conceivable that communities of celebration will remain, or come to be stuck, in intolerance. In any case, it is worth pointing out that the modern temperament is attuned to the discovery and exposure of communal intolerance.

It is quite insensitive, however, to its own intolerance. Inasmuch as the modern spirit has been embodied in the liberal and technological society, it strongly favors a particular style of life and tends to suffocate alternative ways. In particular, it all but enforces a life divided between public production and private consumption, and it clearly discourages communities of celebration. This is simply to restate earlier points under the heading of intolerance.

Communal intolerance tends to be acute and visibly destructive, while technological intolerance is more implicit, diffused, and insidiously detrimental. The Constitution allows for the vigorous national advancement of technological intolerance through the Interstate Commerce Clause but shows no other reflection of it. If the Constitution contained an explicit provision enjoining maximum growth of the gross national product by every available means, we might be more conscious and critical of our characteristic contemporary intolerance. Still, we should be on our guard against both communal and technological intolerance. This task, among others, must find its place in communal politics, and it leads me to the last major point of this essay.

Without public support, genuine communities of celebration will be impossible, and to secure such support appropriately is the task of communal politics.[56] Public support is needed, for without it communal celebrations will founder on the shoals of marginality, injustice, and instability.

I have discussed the first two perils. Consideration of the third brings us to the center of communal politics. Instability is the fate of communities of celebration when they are entrusted to truly voluntary associations. Liberals favor the latter as vehicles of the good life because they seem both to serve our higher aspirations and to preserve the moral neutrality of the government unsullied. But even if we were to assume that voluntary associations could avoid the straits of marginality and injustice, they would suffer shipwreck on the problem of instability.

As we have seen in the discussion of the Olympics and the restoration of the Statue of Liberty, what seems private and voluntary may well be public and mandatory. Symphony societies with paid staffs and regular corporate contributors are not actually voluntary associations. In a democracy, there are few things of social importance that we can disclaim public responsibility for. An association is voluntary in the liberals' sense only when its members work without or against the implicit support of the government, the support that is given above all through education and the tax laws. Hence, the measure of an association's voluntariness is its dependence on volunteer work. But genuine volunteer work, effort we take out of our own hide, is exhausting. Unless there are ever new groups of volunteers to fill the breach, a truly voluntary association will sooner or later collapse.[57]

Government, to be sure, should not arrogate or preempt the place of genuine voluntary associations. Rather, the task of communal politics is to accept and support explicitly the communities of celebration that already exist or are struggling to be born so that they can assume a central and stable position in the public realm. Public support is not a matter of everything or nothing. There must be a balance between public officials and the officers of voluntary associations. The latter possess a skill of community building that is indispensable.

Some community builders disdain or resent government and take pride in keeping public support and authority at bay. Again, such people deserve respect and liberty, but we should remind them that to give up on government is to give up on an inclusively communal and explicitly responsible common order. Just as government must embrace communal celebration, community building must claim government.

Public support through the government, then, can provide the stability communal celebration requires. But just as community is set between intimacy and anonymity, so stability should be set off against inertia as well as precariousness. Public funding of communities of celebration must remain contestable. It should be stable enough to allow practices of celebration to grow, prosper, and evolve gradually, but each community of celebration should have to explain and prove itself periodically in public hearings or plebiscites.

In exercising the vigilance that stable communities require, communal politics is some third thing between technological and theocratic politics. According to the prevailing pattern of technology, politics is the machinery of last appeal, the governor, as said above, that regulates the vast industrial machinery. Politics today cannot disavow this task, but neither should it be confined to it. Politics needs to serve and represent the deeper aspirations of the people, but it hardly needs saying that people do not worship one divine power whose vicar the government could presume to be. Our time is essentially pluralist, yet we should not allow its pluralism to degenerate into a mere variety of degrees of affluence and styles of consumption. A profound pluralism is realized in a plurality of communal celebrations. It should, moreover, leave room for those who find fulfillment in consumption.

Communal politics cannot constitute or stage national celebrations in the properly communal sense, but it is the forum for the public affirmation of communal celebration. To affirm, in this instance, is to embrace, to foster, and to order. Communal politics must, in analogy to Walzer's view, establish and guard the boundaries of the various communities of celebration. This task will be no less contentious than that of current politics, but the contention will be deeper and more fruitful, and it can certainly lead to nationally shared moments of reflection or days of celebration.[58] Regarding the latter, one might hope not only for a more substantial enactment of our national holidays, but for a sympathetic national sharing of, say, the commemoration of Passover and Ramadan.

Communal politics, at any rate, will lead to a significant physical and moral restructuring of the common order. Let me begin with the physical and conclude this chapter with the moral. There is a widely felt need for the reordering of our built environment.[59] The technological spirit of our times has made any significant attempt in this direction inconceivable apart from a master plan or overall design; this approach typically fails in the face of political inertia or resistance, and where it succeeds, under limited and favorable circumstances, the result is often cold and arid.

There is now a growing public awareness that the Cartesian approach of radical razing and reconstruction is destructive, and that urban renewal requires contextual sensitivity.[60] But there is a danger that renewal gets arrested in simply giving the vast machinery of technology a more pleasant and livable appearance, and that we fail to challenge the dissolution of the truly public spaces into the public instrumentalities of labor, transportation, and shopping, and the private enclaves where, as the chair of a marketing consulting firm tells us, "people are interested in 'cocooning' in comfortable dens."[61]

To recover or establish a public site for communal celebration is to restore public space from instrumentality to finality, from a transportation utility to a dwelling place. This may seem to be a rather bland prescription. The reply is to translate the suggestion into the construction or rehabilitation of parks, plazas, and pedestrian zones; of playing fields, golf courses, and running trails; of amphitheaters, concert halls, and museums; of churches, synagogues, and mosques; all this and more should be entrusted to professional people.[62] It seems clear, at any rate, that if we were to follow this suggestion, there would be a radical change of our economic and public lives.

I come to the moral conclusion. Communities of celebration will breach the wall that technology has erected by dividing the world into public production and private consumption. They would not tear the wall down. Although I share some of the concerns of the radical thinkers who would erase the public-private division, I agree with Jean Bethke Elshtain that our welfare and that of our children require the private realm of the family.[63]

Elsewhere I have argued that we can begin to reform the personal and private sphere of our lives if we center it on focal things and practices.[64] The latter are communal celebrations writ small, celebrations in the smallest communal circle of the family. I think the observation remains valid, but it has been clear from the start that focal concerns which remain confined to the personal realm will remain precarious as well.[65] As long as society at large is centrally and finally technological, it contravenes personal focal practices morally and tangibly; morally by disavowing them in public, tangibly by constantly reducing or eliminating the things and settings a family needs for its focal practice.

Without communities of celebration, familial focal practices furthermore become precarious at the point where the family must let the children venture into the world at large. At that moment, youngsters pass from private focal practices, if this is what we have given them, into a public realm where their communal aspirations now clash with the distracting and solipsistic character of the one "activity" that our culture procures for them: consumption.

Communal consumption is an oxymoron and leads to the peculiarly unstable and perilous leisure of young people, an unhappy mix of cars, drugs, and sex, of videos and junk food. We surrender our children to

61

communal consumption by default and by design. We fail to take responsibility for the decay of vigorous public life. At the same time, we expend energy and ingenuity on the design of consumption goods to make them as alluring and gratifying as possible.

Of course, it is not physically or socially impossible for a girl or a boy of fourteen to continue with a sport, an art, or a religious commitment in a wider and more public setting, and some in fact do. But young people have a fine sense of where the cultural center of gravity lies, what finally carries the society's approval and authority and what does not. Communities of celebration in their presently stunted or marginal states do not usually hold a teenager's interest and loyalty. They do so in the hybrid cases where a community of celebration can serve as a feeder for the professional entertainment industry. Parental ambition and unrealistic expectations inspire intense work and competition to groom football heroes or pop stars. This subversion of community reminds us that the communal spirit needs nurture and protection. In this endeavor, society needs to follow the instruction of the kind of feminism that has rightly pointed out that women, for whatever reason, are the bearers of the better part of our culture, of a spirit of nurture, care, and connectedness.[66] I suggest that feminism and celebration require one another. Careful feminism needs a way of extending its heritage and concern into a real and public setting. Celebration needs compassion and sharing if it is to be sustainable and avoid the intoxication of imperious and invidious competitiveness. If we are able to establish and sustain truly public and communal celebrations, we will enable our children to pass in a more secure and salutary way from the family into the wider world.

What makes the world difficult for the kinds of lives we desire for our children is not only the allure of affluence and consumption, but also a widespread attitude of transparency and control. That orientation draws illicit support from the sciences, but is explicitly embraced by technology. Its object of attack is, in any case, the region of contingent and unforethinkable events—the realm that is also the precinct of habitual grace.

Part 2 ■

The Place
of Christianity in the
Culture of Technology

4 ◼

Contingency
and Grace

M any of us share the intuition that contemporary life is uniquely
inhospitable to Christianity. What makes this unreceptive atmosphere unique is its general lack of apparent opposition. Our culture
seems indifferent to the real message of Christianity and at the same
time is eroding the ground that Christianity needs to prosper. There are
head-on attempts at bringing Christian doctrine to bear on the life of
our society, such as branding our culture as materialist, trying to promote prayer in school through legislation, and seeking to outlaw abor-
tion. But for all their directness, these attempts appear to have little purchase on the deeply underlying problem. Something less direct and
more reflective is called for.

A first step in this direction is to recognize that the indifference of
contemporary culture to Christianity is, theologically speaking, a problem of grace, of God's presence in our world. A second step is to raise
the philosophical question (or the question of fundamental theology,
natural theology, or apologetics) regarding receptivity to grace in our
society. Grace is always undeserved and often unforethinkable, and a
culture of transparency and control systematically reduces, if it does not
occlude, the precinct of grace. A technical term for what lies beyond
prediction and control is contingency. What we need to recover then as
a condition of receiving grace is the realm of significant contingency.

The kind of approach to reality that aims at transparency and control is but another definition of modern technology. Thus our task comes to securing in a reasonable and principled way a realm of substantial contingency in the culture of technology. But if we want to be equal to the full force of our task—examining and readying the conditions for the reception of grace—we must consider it not only in the relatively local setting of technological culture but also in the global conditions of evolution and cosmology.

If that looks like an impossibly big and ambitious task, we can take uneasy comfort from the fact that physicists, biologists, and philosophers (I will consider at least one in each category) have focused the problem sharply and concluded: "No contingency, therefore no divinity." If technology is inhospitable to Christianity in being indifferent to it, scientists reject religion and theology by dismissing them. Here too the head-on approach by way of inviting theologians and scientists to a dialogue has had limited success. Focusing on contingency provides a more reflective strategy and reveals at least some common ground. In any event, we have to make sure, within reasonable limits, that the contingency we aim to wrest from technology is not shown to be illusory by cosmology and biology.

What really has to bother us right at the start is the fact that the majority of scientists are not religious. To be precise, 60 percent of scientists generally are atheists or agnostics. If that worries us, the fact that the more prominent a scientist is the less likely he or she is to be religious should concern us even more. Of the elite that is gathered in the National Academy of Sciences, 90 percent are atheist or agnostic. The least religious among NAS scientists are the biologists. Only 5 percent of them believe in God and an afterlife.

In an effort to narrow the gap between religion and science, physicists have been invited to discuss their disagreements with religion and theology, but their dismissal of both is so profound that nothing fruitful seems to be left to disagree about. "You clearly can be a scientist and have religious beliefs," said British chemist Peter Atkins. He continued: "But I don't think you can be a real scientist in the deepest sense of the word, because they are such alien categories of knowledge."[1] American physicist Steven Weinberg has put it more pointedly yet:

> I am all in favor of a dialogue between science and religion, but not a constructive dialogue. One of the great achievements of science has been, if not to make it impossible for intelligent people to be religious, then at

least to make it possible for them not to be religious. We should not retreat from this accomplishment.[2]

The depth of disagreement has led British philosopher Rosalind Hursthouse (who, ever so cautiously, professes theism) to think of the disagreement as located in an area

> where 'argument breaks down' at least in the sense that intelligent and even philosophically very sophisticated people exist on both sides of the debate, fully conversant with each others' arguments and completely unshaken by them. All the Christians and atheists I know think that the people on the other side are just plain wrong, but that there is no 'sort of discussion or exploration which might, given the particular subject matter' lead either side out of error.[3]

Hursthouse's resignation is no less worrisome than the scientists' contempt. It implies that rational inquiry and religious doctrine cannot consist with one another.[4]

To reach an area of more articulate disagreement we can turn to the problem of contingency, and to get a firmer grip on contingency we must remember that reality is a texture of laws and conditions. The laws tell us what in general is possible. The actual conditions embody the laws in a particular situation. Take the weather. The laws of physics tell us that precipitation will fall down rather than up, that it turns into ice crystals below 32° Fahrenheit, that cold air is denser or heavier than warm air, and so on. But for meteorologists to predict the weather they need to know, ideally, all the conditions that prevail today and, ideally, everywhere; and the laws plus the conditions in the ideal case would permit an accurate prediction of how the weather will turn out tomorrow, next week, and for the next several months. To illuminate an object or event by finding out how it is governed by scientific laws constitutes the model of explanation in the modern era, and controlling a phenomenon by varying some of its lawfully governed conditions is the wellspring of technological power.

Contingency is found both in laws and in conditions. As to laws, contingency pertains to their origin and to their parameters, that is, to those constants that restrict an overly general law to the way our world actually is. Regarding conditions, it is their ultimate origin and their present meaning that are contingent. In the advancement of modern science, the discovery of a law is a gain in the transparency of the world, especially when a law or lawful explanation illuminates the previously brute givenness of conditions. The work of Newton illustrates both of these points.

Alexander Pope captured the illuminating force of Newtonian theory in the couplet,

> Nature and Nature's laws lay hid in night.
> God said, "Let Newton be!" and all was light.

Well, not quite all. Newton himself thought that certain cosmic conditions were simply unexplainable. He held "that the motions which planets now have could not spring from any natural cause alone, but were impressed by an intelligent Agent."[5] In Newton's inference we can see a first explicit tie between contingency and divinity. Where explanation ends, God begins to appear. Conversely, where contingency is reduced or eliminated, theophany dissolves.

Today's cosmology has an explanation for the orbits of the planets.[6] When cosmic matter coagulates in a star, a rotating disc of stuff under certain conditions forms around the star, and in time the disc breaks up and concentrates into the clumps we call planets. It follows that planets will revolve in the same plane and direction around a star. Thus contingency yields to explanation.

Laws, moreover, not only reduce contingency and theophany, rather their necessity and universality seem to lend them unquestionable and self-sufficient force and appear to obviate the question of their origin. Henry Adams, a hypersensitive observer of the rise of contemporary culture, felt the sovereignty of lawful explanation when he was confronted with Darwinian evolution:

> Natural Selection led back to Natural Evolution and at last to Natural Uniformity. This was a vast stride. Unbroken Evolution under uniform conditions pleased every one—except curates and bishops; it was the very best substitute for religion; a safe, conservative, practical, thoroughly Common-Law deity.[7]

Newton, of course, thought that contingency gave God a place *within* lawfulness. But when lawfulness more and more explains and eliminates divine intervention, physicists eventually, as Laplace memorably put it to Napoleon, "have no need of that hypothesis."[8]

The contingency of conditions and their theological implications have had a recent revival, however. John Leslie has been its most impressive champion. He has pointed out that, while some contingencies have been explained away, others have resisted, such as the force of gravity, which in principle can assume indefinitely many different values without invalidating the general consistency of the law of which it is a part. But not only is the force of gravity an unexplainable given, it also needs to have a value that is precise to one part in 10^{100}—an unimaginably fine tuning—for a universe with intelligent life to be possible, one that neither expands nor contracts "furiously" and leaves time for evolution.[9]

This along with many other fine tunings in astrophysics, impressively laid out by Leslie, has resurrected the argument from design, and it is one of the creditable head-on replies to scientific atheism. As we should expect, however, atheists are not out of rejoinders. There are principally two. One is to point out that astrophysics is very much in flux and that the hoped for final theory will be free of all contingent quantities.[10] The other is to posit a multiverse of infinitely many different universes one of which has to exhibit the values that the evolution of intelligent life requires, and that universe happens to be ours.

In reply, a theist can appeal to the ultimate contingency that surfaces in the questions, "Why is there a multiverse? Why is there something rather than nothing?" Instead of the many contingencies that have impressed Leslie, there is the one great contingency of the existence of reality that is explained by the existence of a Creator God. Yet again there is an atheist reply. Weinberg puts it this way:

> If that's true, what explains that? Why is there such a God? It isn't the end of the chain of whys, it is just another step, and you have to take the step beyond that.[11]

Richard Dawkins, a biologist, has it less diplomatically (and at a lower level of contingency though the force of his argument bears on any level):

> This is a transparently feeble argument, indeed it is obviously self-defeating. . . . To explain the origin of the DNA/protein machine by invoking a supernatural Designer is to explain precisely nothing, for it leaves unexplained the origin of the Designer. You have to say something like "God was always there," and if you allow yourself that kind of lazy way out, you might as well just say "DNA was always there," or "Life was always there," and be done with it.[12]

Daniel Dennett, the philosopher, finally, makes the point with characteristic wit and irreverence:

69

If God created all these wonderful things, who created God? Supergod? And who created Supergod? Superdupergod? Or did God create himself? Was it hard work? Did it take time? Don't ask![13]

The origin and the existence of the world and its lawful structure turn out to be contingent since they have no explanation. But it seems to be a pale and silent contingency, and a scientist may reasonably argue that, once the best current explanation of the universe has been given, we may well press for a still better explanation but cannot plausibly demand an explanation of the explanation. The chain of explanations has to end somewhere. Do Christians have an answer to that?

A creditable reply can be found when we turn from the contingency of laws to that of conditions. They are by definition simply given, and no explanation whatever is available. In some cases the contingency of today's conditions can be explained through recourse to yesterday's. But at some point the causal chains seem to trail off in complexity or happenstance.

Recent discoveries have very much heightened the contingency of conditions, for they have shown that in certain kinds of physical settings arbitrarily small differences in the initial conditions lead, within certain limits, to vastly different results. This is not at all what we, heirs to Newton, have learned to expect. A small difference in the angle of a cannon will make the cannonball land in a slightly different place. But the disturbance of the air movement contributed by the notorious butterfly in Brazil can make the difference between sunshine and a hurricane in Florida's subsequent weather. The problem, however, is not just *small* differences but *arbitrarily* small differences—differences however small. Thus the initial state of these remarkable systems will forever elude determination since our instruments and methods of measurement have a floor of precision, and the crucial factors will always lie below the floor. The systems in question are fully determined by the laws of physics, but their initial conditions cannot be ascertained. These systems are deterministic *and* unpredictable. They are instances of deterministic chaos so called. The well-known example of such a system's behavior is of course the weather. Here is contingency, sometimes with a vengeance.

The opponent of contingency might reply that this is not contingency in principle but a merely practical problem. The atmosphere and the weather are in principle explainable. It is the practical limits of measurement that keep us from explaining and predicting the weather with precision and over the long term. To this Stephen H. Kellert replies: "Chaos theory . . . challenges the very distinction between theoretical and practical impossibility."[14]

Here we come to the second explicit tie between contingency and divinity. John Polkinghorne finds in this indeterminacy the opening for divine intervention.[15] Though I broadly agree with Polkinghorne, his proposal too may be taken as patently unacceptable to the atheist. As if to strike a preemptive blow against Polkinghorne's position, Kellert, a philosopher of science pretty much in the classical tradition, has said: "But any expectation that chaos theory will re-enchant the world will be met with disappointment."[16]

Dawkins has tried to provide a general argument why the disenchantment of the world and the deflation of contingency are unavoidable. His argument rests on a certain interpretation of Darwin's theory. Contingency looms large in evolution, and how a proponent of it sees contingency has a bearing on his or her attitude toward religion or theology. A third, somewhat less explicit, tie between divinity and contingency comes to the surface here. To appreciate it, we need to supply some background.

For Stephen J. Gould contingency is a source of wonder, and accordingly, we may infer, he respects religion and has proposed

that we encapsulate this central principle of respectful noninterference—accompanied by intense dialog between the two distinct subjects—by enunciating the Principle of Noma, or Non-Overlapping Magisteria.[17]

Dennett, to the contrary, is bent on ultimately emptying contingency of any meaning whatever, and not surprisingly, we may again conclude, he subscribes to Ronald de Sousa's quip that philosophical theology is "intellectual tennis without a net."[18]

For Dawkins the beginning of evolutionary biology is awe at the intricacy of life. He admires William Paley who in 1802 likened this intricacy to that of a watch and drove "his point home with beautiful and reverent descriptions of the dissected machinery of life . . . ," Dawkins says, and for his part he stresses that

one thing I shall not do is belittle the wonder of the living "watches" that so inspired Paley. On the contrary, I shall try to illustrate my feeling that here Paley could have gone even further. When it comes to feeling awe over living "watches" I yield to nobody.[19]

Yet for Dawkins such awe is tentative and finally mistaken. He tells us

that one of my aims in the book is to convey something of the sheer wonder of biological complexity to those whose eyes have not been opened

71

to it. But having built up the mystery, my other main aim is to remove it again by explaining the solution.[20]

But, as I want to show later, this violation of the conservation of reverence involves an illicit switch from one kind of response to another.

There are many kinds of contingent things and events. They range from the trivial and negligible to those that have a commanding presence. Remarkably, Weinberg, Dennett, and Dawkins all pay tribute to the latter kind. For Weinberg, the classic beauty of certain physical theories is nothing less than "compelling."[21] Even more so is the "messy" beauty of art.[22] "I love grand opera," he has said. "I can't hear 'La Bohème' without dissolving."[23]

Dennett in the very first section of his great book on *Darwin's Dangerous Idea* raises the question, "Is Nothing Sacred?" and promises to show "how what really matters to us—and ought to matter to us—shines through, transformed but enhanced by its passage through the Darwinian Revolution."[24] And toward the end of the book he emphatically repeats the question and the answer: "Is something sacred? Yes, I say with Nietzsche. I could not pray to it, but I can stand in affirmation of its magnificence. This world is sacred."[25]

Dawkins is most emphatic on this point though he takes it back in the end. Weinberg and Dennett evidently want to sustain the commanding presence of scientific theory, of art, and of nature though both labor under a tension if not inconsistency. For Weinberg the beauty of theory and art is embedded in a chillingly impersonal and pointless universe.[26] In Dennett's universe, contingency is ultimately random. The reality, though not the origin and shape, of meaning has always been an open question in Dennett's work.[27]

At any rate, in the commanding presence that contingency can have lies something like an answer, or at least a reasonable outline of an answer, to the question of the origin and existence of the world. Weinberg's reactions to the beauty of nature and art are most telling in this regard. He has this to say about the beauty of nature:

> I have to admit that sometimes nature seems more beautiful than strictly necessary. Outside the window of my home office there is a hackberry tree, visited frequently by a convocation of politic birds: blue jays, yellow-throated vireos, and loveliest of all, an occasional red cardinal. Although I understand pretty well how brightly colored feathers evolved out of a competition for mates, it is almost irresistible to imagine that all this beauty was somehow laid on for our benefit.[28]

As far as the beauty of art is concerned, Weinberg is reported to be "deeply touched by music and poetry in ways he admits reason can never justify or explain."[29]

Evidently reality can address us in different ways—in its causal references or in its commanding presence. Accordingly reality can provoke curiosity, research, and analysis or appreciation, admiration, and reverence. These two modes of being (and our replies to them) are consistent with one another, and they coincide with the warp and weft of reality—laws and conditions. Reality described as a web of laws and conditions is seen from everywhere and nowhere. Reality seen as presence within a net of reference is acknowledged here and now. Everything has presence and reference if not always in equal measure. But the two kinds of existence should not be mistaken for one another, as they are by Dawkins, nor should our kinds of responses be confused with each other, the way Dawkins confuses them. The coloration of feathers elicits curiosity in the ornithologist and admiration in the birder. Curiosity is restless and endless. Reverence finds peace and affirmation in its object. Analogously the Creator God is offered by theists not as an object of curiosity and a causal factor—creation is donation not causation—but rather is called upon as the Commanding Presence simply, properly met with the response Weinberg, Dawkins (at least initially), and Dennett extend to nature and art.

These two modes of being—reference and presence—and the appropriate responses—curiosity and reverence—furnish the outlines for what has happened in the culture at large since the beginning of modern technology and for what needs to be done now. Reference and presence have modes of contingency that they share respectively with laws and conditions. Accordingly it is the contingency of presence that is the more impressive and disclosive one. As it turns out, though this contingency is undeniable, it is not irreducible. In fact we can read modern history as the restless and endless assault on contingency, a process that at length has occluded the presence of things and haunted the peace of humans. Accordingly our task comes to restoring the eloquent contingency of nature and culture and recovering the spirit of reverence.

The point of all this is finally not cultural but theological and religious though the cultural concern is creditable enough and constitutes common ground with many atheists. A helpful focus of the shared terrain is the notion of grace, in both its secular and religious varieties. To begin with secular grace, Weinberg softens and warms his hard and chilling account of the universe by concluding his first popular (I would say "philosophical") book with the sentence: "The effort to understand the universe is one of the very few things that lifts human life a little above the level of farce, and gives it some of the grace of tragedy."[30] John Rawls concludes his magnificent *Theory of Justice* by considering the whole-hearted acceptance of the principles of justice. "Purity of heart," he says, "if one could attain it, would be to see clearly and to act with grace and self-command from this point of view."[31] A graceful life corresponds to the region of contingency that is the common concern of Christians and thoughtful atheists.

Christians, to be sure, are less than confident that they can secure all by themselves any measure of grace, but are much more confident that grace can become fully realized and does so as the gift of God, lifting us above tragedy and healing our frailty. But that confidence needs to be examined and reaffirmed in light of the erosion of its ground through modern technology. Divine grace, of course, has not become question-able across the board, else its predicament would have escaped no one. Hence we need to distinguish between kinds of grace.

Sacramental grace, the blessing Christians receive in communal wor-ship, is not in question though it is in danger of diminishment through the technological attack on commanding presence. *Actual grace*—a ges-ture of forgiveness, the stillness of nature, the consolations of music—descends where it will though it is frequently confused with its coun-terfeit version—grace as a ticket to success. Karl Rahner throughout his life pleaded for a still wider and deeper understanding of the presence of God's benevolence and beneficence. Grace, he urged, is fundamen-tally not God's episodic intervention in history and the occasional ele-vation of the human soul, but the omnipresent goodness of salvation that every human being is capable of realizing. He calls this existential grace a "supernatural *a priori*."[32] I will call it *universal grace*. To Rahner's argument I will add an underlining of the fact that universal grace has in each epoch of history a characteristic habit or appearance and, par-ticularly in the information age, a kind of disappearance and conceal-ment as well. That disappearance is most advanced in the affluent indus-trial countries. I will call historically qualified universal grace *habitual grace*.

Habitual grace provides the habitat for actual grace, but only in a gen-eral sort of way since grace can break into a person's life no matter the cultural ecology of a particular time. Still, the shape of historical con-tingency bears on what actually happens in life. Consider the actually twofold grace of traditional misery. If in the days before vaccination your

74

children contracted smallpox and three of the six died, the survival of three was a joyful gift of grace, gratefully received, while the death of the other three brought consoling grace, much more difficult to realize, of course. At least in some cases, the moment of crisis between life and death was one of what John Polkinghorne has called the "particular critical points at which divine influence was exercised in particular ways," and at the same time one of those, as Polkinghorne has it, that "would be scientifically indiscernible, veiled within the cloudy nature of the event in question."[33]

It might have been a case of the deterministic chaos Kellert has discussed. But evidently we can preempt and overpower the elusive conditions of an infection through vaccination just as, more obviously, we can tame the chaotic water flow of a mountain stream through a pipeline and as we can fix the course of a plane through the chaotic medium of the atmosphere. Very often we can enforce what Kellert has called "clock work hegemony."[34] Thus we eliminate in fact the "critical points at which divine influence was exercised." Should we restore those occasions of actual grace?

For theoretical reasons, no doubt, rather than religious ones, a French anthropologist, as Martha Nussbaum reports, has expressed "regret that the introduction of smallpox vaccination to India by the British eradicated the cult of Sittala Devi, the goddess to whom one used to pray in order to avert smallpox." To which Nussbaum sensibly replied "that it is surely better to be healthy rather than ill, to live rather than to die."[35]

There is no question for us mainstream Christians that the contingencies of childhood disease and death, of starvation following bad harvests, of freezing in winter for lack of fuel, proper shelter, or clothing, of confinement due to lack of transportation, and of ignorance because of a dearth of information, that all these contingencies are gone for better rather than worse. And this evident moral fact greatly complicates the task of recovering a region of contingency and habitual grace.

Approaching the problem more generally and historically we find that the first phase of the technological assault on contingency began with the Industrial Revolution in the late eighteenth century and lasted roughly through the nineteenth. It mounted a successful attack on the basic conditions and needs of life—space, time, food, shelter, public health, education, and information. An emblem of this development is the steam engine. It freed the availability of power from the vagaries of wind and water and, for the first time since the taming of the horse, extended the reach and speed of transportation through the locomotive.

75

The building of the railroads is the most incisive instance of early technological progress. It also shows that in the first phase of modern technology the contingencies of miseries and blessings changed but did not disappear. People were injured and died through falls from scaffoldings, explosions of boilers, collapses of mine shafts, and similarly brutal causes. To us, the indifference to human health and safety in the initial conquest of nature looks appalling. Still, the general balance of the technological enterprise moved toward the exclusion of accidents and calamities. That trend is well illustrated by Josiah Royce's reaction to the first continental railroad. Speaking of the newly accessible California, he said: "The region that to-day is so swiftly and easily entered was of old the goal of an overland tour that might easily last six months from the Missouri River, and that was attended with many often-recorded dangers."[36]

The technological liberation from toil and misery was then and is still being regarded as freeing a space and the time for human flourishing. What has most always been overlooked is the fact that technology has not only made room for pleasure but has also invaded and occupied the liberated space and has impressed its particular shape on our typical enjoyments. To be sure, the advancement of technology did not move from the conquest of necessities and calamities to the procurement of pleasures and luxuries by crossing a clear dividing line. The region of needs and the region of wants overlapped and dovetailed in many ways. Still the major thrust of the second phase of technology occurred in the middle and the second half of the twentieth century.

Technology by itself, of course, did nothing. It merely constituted a pattern that people in the industrial countries have devised, developed, and applied everywhere. The pattern exhibits the familiar conjunction of mechanization and commodification. Mechanization is the invention of some machinery that takes over the toils and burdens of providing some good, and the good, freed from its natural encumbrances, social burdens, and cultural ties, becomes available as a commodity for purchase and consumption. Thus the machinery of the phonograph assumed the onus of providing music, and music became available in the shape of records that could be bought and played wherever and whenever. Thus a technological device exhibits paradigmatically the tight and distinctive connection of machinery and commodity. The canonical response to commodities, finally, is consumption. Thus the joint effects of mechanization, commodification, and consumption transformed traditional cultures from the ground up.

The effect of this campaign was to constrict actual grace in its personal and real variants. Coaxing children to learn an instrument and prevailing on musicians to convene for domestic celebrations requires grace on our part. But making music transforms us into recipients as well as bearers of grace as when a fine trio provokes delight and gratitude. Analogously, strolling through town on a summer's evening makes for pleasure and thankfulness at the sight of handsome buildings and gracious parks. All this has been greatly reduced and often eliminated through the devices of radio, stereo, and television.

In the last quarter-century, information technology has perfected and begun to complete tendencies that have been long in developing. The drift away from public and civic involvement began after the Second World War and has since gained momentum as Robert Putnam has vividly and exhaustively shown.[37] What has spurred this development is its attractive force. The shape it takes looks much like the cell E. M. Forster has described in "The Machine Stops"—a secluded place of great comfort and limitless media.[38] All the world is at one's call and beckon, and hence to venture out into the world begins to feel like a waste and a pain.

The perfection of the domestic cocoon is proceeding through the proliferation and improvement of information devices—extended telephone service, digital television with large screens, personal computers and the entirety of cyberspace they open up. Information technology, moreover, is insinuating itself into the very structure of our homes to disburden us from having to worry about our lights, our warmth, our safety, our food supplies, and more.

What is even more remarkable and goes beyond or against Forster's dystopian vision is the extension of domestic comfort and control to the globe entire. Not so long ago you needed a map and careful observation, and preferably a quick and alert companion, to find an unfamiliar address, and many times you still had to stop at a gas station to seek help. Now with a technological guide supported by the global positioning system, a gentle voice tells you what exactly is coming and precisely where to turn. There are GPS devices that will similarly guide you through trackless wilderness.

As a result, the commanding presence of things is yielding to a semblance of transparent omniscience and omnipresence. Things no longer occupy a place and take their time. To see what is going on in the city of my youth, I no longer have to cross a continent and an ocean to find it in its place, rather Web sites and Web cameras show and tell me at an instant what I want to see and know. The etherealized presence of Freiburg is further attenuated by the copresence in cyberspace of hundreds of other cities and sites and by the possibility of penetrating the visual surface of towns and countries to lay bare their geology, hydrography, ecology, population patterns, economic structure, transportation networks, and more. The ultimate dissolution of real presence is achieved in virtual realities where pervasive intelligibility implodes into total control by designers if not also by players.

To the dissolution of commanding reality corresponds on the human side a peculiar restlessness. Since every item of cyberpresence can be x-rayed, zoomed into, overlayed, and abandoned for another more promising site, human desire is at every point at once satiated, disappointed, and aroused to be once more gorged, left hungry, and spurred on. This restlessness takes characteristically distinct forms in the mental and emotional economy of the elites and of the middle class, with many kinds of hybrids in between. The well trained and driven go from task to task in endless pursuit of fame and fortune while the less skilled and less ambitious surf the sea of television and cyberspace and, in the case of the more prosperous middle class, hop from one tourist attraction to another with no coherence or history to connect one Web site or sunny beach with another.

This world without time, place, and grace is attractive or at least seductive in its own ways and, more important, has shown great staying power. Hence we, who deplore it, cannot sit back to await its collapse and to be called on for help. We must meet its seductiveness with the good news of Christ and its durability with conviction. One way of getting our bearing for this enterprise is to return to the root of the technological promise—the eradication of trouble from the human condition. Trouble is often the twin of grace, and if one cannot prosper, neither can the other. Roger Scruton has pilloried the moral debacle that follows the suppression of trouble:

> If we believe that the state is there to cushion us from misfortune, to compensate every loss and make up for every suffering, then we automatically relinquish control over our lives, while drastically narrowing the sphere of human action. Regulations of a mind-numbing complexity now govern activities, consumer products, and employment, with the aim of ensuring that the citizen can amble through a risk-free world, picking his pleasures from shelves loaded with packaged and sanitized products, waddling onwards in a state of moral obesity.[39]

It may be a sign of the gravity of our condition that a conservative British philosopher like Scruton and the politically hypercorrect French anthropologist pilloried by Nussbaum are driven to gesture at the same desperate remedy—maintaining trouble and misery.

The first step toward a morally acceptable and theologically sensible recovery of contingency is to distinguish between trouble we reject in principle but accept in practice and trouble we accept in practice and in principle. When cancer strikes or a car crashes, we should resist the uncomprehending anger that rises from the culture of transparency and control and instead pray for the grace that allows us to accept what has come our way. I realize that we brush up against the problem of evil and the theodicy here. The sole point I want to stress is that these problems are hard or impossible to solve from a third person declarative point of view but are not so from a first person performative standpoint. If I find consoling grace, the evil before me, my evil, no longer cries out for explanation or revenge. Such acceptance, however, is quite compatible with pressing for cancer research and greater highway safety.

When it comes to the trouble of cooking a meal and gathering my loved ones around the table, we accept it not only in practice but also in principle because eating, shorn of its real preparation and personal involvements, has lost its sacramental horizon. Similarly, the trouble of getting up early, driving to the trail head, and, most important, the pain and panting of a steep ascent are the irreplaceable ways the imposing elevation of a mountain is realized. And trouble of that sort, finally, is required to make attendance at a local concert the rich and rewarding event it often is.

Often, but not always. Common meals can be bitter, hikes in the mountains calamitous, and concerts embarrassing. It lies in the nature of grace that we do not command it but certainly can and often do turn it away. There is no guarantee of real grace in city and country nor in common meals and actual concerts. But there is a definite occlusion of such grace in the cocoon of self-indulgence.

In concert with all people of goodwill we must work to institute the habitual grace that allows real and personal grace more often to be realized today. This "we must" is the response to an enormous enlargement of Peter's commission (Matt. 16:19). The kingdom whose keys are entrusted to us now includes all there is in terrestrial heaven and earth, and it is up to us whether we reduce it all to resources and utilities or can muster the reverence that is required to help it retain or regain its characteristic face and its own voice. The habitat of real grace is the place where reverence and personal grace can be realized. Thus there is a conjunction of real and personal grace. The fate of real grace today lies in the hands of humans while humans can lead deeply graceful lives only in a graceful world.

There seems to be a circle of actual and habitual grace, one grace presupposing the other—a phenomenon reminiscent of the ancient question whether grace is required to receive grace. If that circle threatens us with helplessness, there is another that can trap us in ill-conceived power. We are drawn into that circle when we decide to confront trouble unconditionally and then get caught in the desolation of thoughtlessness. There is a theoretical and a practical side to this predicament. The theoretical side is the burden of theology when in dealing with the problem of technology we turn to technological standards of success. The practical side is our complicity with the technological strategy of demanding results regardless of circumstances. Both sides and circles break open, however, when we let go of regardless power and recognize that genuine power, careful power, is something we receive rather than produce.

5 ▪

Power and Care

The task of a theology of technology is to grasp the relationship of Christianity and technology both profoundly and fruitfully. It is worth reminding ourselves that such theology is part of a long and distinctive tradition. Once Christians recognized as remarkable a truth that was not revealed—the truth of nature or of history—and as soon as they began to reflect on such truth in a principled way, they gave birth to something like a natural or fundamental theology. Fundamental theology today must be a theology of technology, the successor to medieval natural theology.

By a different path the student of technology may also be led to something like theology. What a reflective turn to technology experiences readily, and finally in exasperation, is the endless variety and articulation of technology. Philosophers have in large part stayed away from an examination of modern technology for so long not because there is so little to say about it but too much. Since it is a novel and concrete phenomenon, the guidance of the tradition or of professional discipline is not available. The consequent disorientation affords a forceful invitation to reflect on questions of what really and finally matters, and such questions may open one to matters of ultimate concern.

A good starting point for a theology of technology is everyday culture in the United States. It is the oldest among the advanced industrial siblings since it is always the first to pass through the stages of modern or postmodern technology. It was the first to have an automobile economy, the first to have a television culture, and the first to settle cyberspace

81

via the Internet. From a look at the ways in which technology has infected and transformed all cultures of the globe it appears that there is hope for a coming to terms with technology not in the vortex of the initial confrontation, but only after one has passed through it. It is well to note that, passing through technology, the theology of technology may be as much a transformation as a continuation of traditional fundamental theology.[1]

The latter is clearly the offspring of Platonic and Aristotelian metaphysics. Assuming that Martin Heidegger is right in seeing technology as the final phase of metaphysics, the passage through technology should let us see beyond the ways in which metaphysics has informed Christianity.[2] This does not mean that Christianity allowed itself to be metaphysically corrupted in late Antiquity and in the Middle Ages. All it means is that metaphysics has come to an end in technology and that we are called to another beginning. The call is, however, barely audible and, as we will see, the tendency to fall back into the bondage of traditional voices is strong.

Accordingly, a radical theology of technology would be one that, through the experience of technology, could call into question what now counts as unproblematic, or what is commonly taken as evidence or justification for some claim. In so doing it would help us listen to the word of Christ in a new way. In short I believe that the experience of technology can awaken in us a new *potentia oboedientialis*, a new capacity to hear the word of God.[3]

What then does technology teach us to hear? To find the answer we must first allow technology to come clearly into view. To achieve this it is not necessary to enter into lengthy discussions of how technology is best defined. Our pretheoretical intuition that technology is the human enterprise that somehow distinguishes our time is a sufficient guide. And if Christianity is something that matters to us ultimately, we are already pointed toward what is pervasive and consequential in technology. Still, to catch sight of technology in its wholeness and significance is a difficult task. Technology is so deeply ingrained in our world and our ways that critical endeavors are typically deflected from technology as such to problems within technology; and what is worse, the internal problems then come to be criticized by technological standards.

Problems internal to technology are not necessarily local or partial problems, but rather ones that are recognized as both serious and tractable by a proponent of technology. One example of such an internal critique of technology is provided by Bernard Lonergan as presented by Terry J. Tekippe. Lonergan takes an initially positive view of the creative and productive power of technology, seen as the exercise of intelligence and common sense, but he believes that technology lacks final orientation and security. Technology is finally shortsighted and unenlightened; it fails to take a long-range view, and it is unable to achieve an integration of the countervailing and conflicting forces. Thus it suffers progressive deterioration and courts the danger of a fatal collapse.[4] Environmentalists and Marxists could not agree more. A similar example can be seen in George W. Shields's account of Charles Hartshorne's view of technology. Like Lonergan, Hartshorne attempts to locate the limits of technology and finds them in its inability to provide total freedom from boredom, fear, and uncertainty, to control its detrimental side effects, and to guarantee endless life.[5] But obviously such reproaches do not question the direction in which technology is moving or the character of that movement; they simply criticize technology for not having gone and in fact not being able to go far enough to satisfy us.

The position of Lonergan, Hartshorne, and their spokesmen is so common and so debilitating to a principled critique of technology that it deserves a name of its own. I will call it the "unwarranted optimism of the pessimists." People like Lonergan and Hartshorne intuitively find something profoundly distressing in technology, and consequently they see an urgent need for its reform. Their distress is expressed as a deep pessimism about the prospects of technology; but their apprehension fails to break through the commonplace view of what constitutes success. They adopt technological standards and see technology failing by its own criteria. And this allows them to be optimistic about the necessity, the likelihood, and the nature of a reform of technology. Technology will have to reform itself. The alternative is an overt and imminent technological failure or catastrophe, or so the optimistic pessimists claim. But if it turns out that technology is a self-correcting and self-preserving enterprise, the pessimism is unwarranted—and so ultimately is the optimism. Part of this optimism is the belief that technology, coming to the end of its rope, will have to turn to Christianity for guidance if it is to avoid self-destruction.

What is at issue here is in part an empirical question that cannot be dealt with in one brief sally. But as recent publications by Bill Joy and Francis Fukayama attest, the crisis of technology has the attention of the public, and given this attention, problems will at least be contained and are likely to be solved.[6] But the issue has a theoretical side as well, one that is more unsettling. It indicates that Christian standards have entered into competition with technological ones, and this in turn shows that technology has become such a profoundly established pattern that we now measure Christianity against it. If a more profound critique and reform of technology are possible, one must act on that possibility. To that end, and to avoid final entrapment by technology, we must grasp it as a whole and undertake a total critique.

The crucial issue concerns the vantage point from which technology as a whole might disclose its character. If the location of that privileged place has remained hidden from theologians and philosophers, it is not because that locus is too distant or concealed, but because it is so close and plain. It is easy to find if only we are willing to follow the purposive arrows that are built into the technological system, no matter how complex and multifarious it may seem. In the common understanding it is clear what exists for the sake of what, what further purpose the latter object serves, and so on till the question "What for?" becomes finally inapplicable and the chain of purposes comes to its end. In this network of purposive references, even such a seemingly monumental affair as the launching of a space shuttle is but a penultimate and passing phase. The launch serves to install and maintain satellites. The latter sustain and increase our ability to send electronic signals, and these in turn will convey television programs such as *Friends*. And while all what-for questions antecedent to *Friends* have clear and crisp answers, the replies to "What do people watch *Friends* for?" will be vague and evasive and so indicate that we have come to the foreground and center of technology. The space shuttle is of course connected to many other lines in the network of purposes. It is used for scientific experiments. It repairs weather and land survey satellites. But if in those cases we persist in asking what those endeavors and devices are for, we will again be finally referred to the foreground and center of commodities available for consumption.

We can now see how the problems of the technological society that explicitly occupy Lonergan or Hartshorne are, for the most part, either located in the background of technology or at any rate leave the foreground of consumption unquestioned. At first this lack of attention does not seem an oversight at all. The foreground of consumption is after all modern life in its most ordinary and daily form, the human condition that everyone always and already knows, that is simply understood and is rightly, it seems, taken for granted. But it is in the dailiness of modern life that technology has become powerful and consequential. To capture and highlight the aspect of our world that is crucial for an under-

84

standing of technology, let me speak of the quotidianity, i.e., the daily and inconspicuous character, of modern life.

Why has the quotidianity of modern life so largely escaped attention and scrutiny? The dominant reason is that from the start it was systematically designed to be unproblematic, to be free of insecurity, of challenges, demands, of conflicting creeds, of pain and misery, of confinement, or toil. How this design was first conceived and how implemented are questions in their own right. The transformation of the world according to this pattern was, however, enormously successful, and at two different levels. It succeeded in creating for the industrial societies a world of ease, comfort, and security; and it was more profoundly successful in establishing its norms as dominant and unquestionable. If the former success was not total, the latter was nearly so. Consequently, the critics of technology typically inquire how well technology has done by its own norms. But why should we challenge the technological norms of comfort and security?

As a first approximation we might say that the realization of these norms is the cause of the pleasant indifference that people in an advanced technological society show for the Christian message of salvation, though not necessarily for the trappings of the Christian tradition. A promise of salvation seems to have no purchase in a situation where health is secure, food and shelter are unfailingly available, where boredom and unease are countered by sophisticated diversion. But who is responsible for this new outlook on life? The enjoyment of life's amenities does not as a rule spring from daily decisions but is the appropriate response to a universe of technological devices. The crucial question is whether we allow ourselves to drift into the technological universe. Once we accept more or less innocently the pattern of television sets, refrigerators, and microwave ovens, our lives will be patterned by them and lose their need of salvation.

The setting of technological ease and safety still has its imperfections. Disease and depression still set upon us and our loved ones and bring about pain and untimely death. But here technology shows its power most profoundly, for today the normal reaction to misery is anger and incomprehension. To suffer misery is no longer to be reminded of one's fundamental incompleteness and incapacity, but to be scandalized at the senseless remnant of a time long gone. What misery still exists simply delimits the brute and unintelligible periphery of the technological universe, which is well understood in its central security and comfort.

To break through the enclosure of technological culture, we must turn to the inconspicuous closeness of daily life, and to one simple aspect of it. Consider bread. In pretechnological times the sustaining force of our daily bread, *panis noster quotidianus*, was a focal point of wholeness when people were able to break it and eat it together, and a focal point of mortal misery when bad harvests made it unavailable.[7] In the technological society, bread is unfailingly available. And it is so not only year in and year out, but at every moment of the day and night and in the greatest variety of shapes: toast in the morning, hamburger bun at noon, Hostess Twinkies in the afternoon, pizza in the evening. The ubiquitous and instantaneous availability of bread is a manifestation of our total conquest of hunger. We can demonstrate and exercise our domination of hunger at any moment. This rule of total availability does not tolerate even moments of deprivation. A snack is always at hand, and every twinge of hunger is indulged.

But it is not only bread, as a focal object, that has entirely come to be at our disposal. We have similarly learned to dispose of the regular settings and gatherings in which bread was broken and eaten. Increasingly we free ourselves from the demands of meeting at a particular and regular time, of taking our seats in an orderly arrangement, of going through the steps and courses of a traditional meal. I am reluctant to burden others with rituals, and I prefer to be free of obligations in turn. I eat when it is convenient to my working hours and as it agrees with my taste for entertainment. Breakfast is when one gets up. Lunch depends on the office routine. Dinner is arranged to accommodate or accompany busy lives and a variegated television schedule. What becomes visible in the case of eating is but a part of the broadest pattern of modern quotidianity. Everything is procured for our call and beckon: distant and exotic places, historical events, personal and sexual experiences, stories, songs, and games. As a consequence, there is a glamorous semblance of prosperity and liberty. There is an aura of magic when a new and still more effortless and sparkling form of transportation, communication, or entertainment becomes available. It is magic that must be paid for, of course, through labor. That bargain is well understood and accepted if not highly valued. And it is a compact from which, for all we know, automation may increasingly release us.

Yet underneath that glamour, the darker pattern of our incapacity begins to appear. In the modern universe of abundance and availability our contact with the world is reduced to effortless and inconsequential consumption. The availability of commodities is necessarily accompanied by a loss of depth and disclosure of what once occupied the place of the commodity. The loss of depth is a sober and prosaic phenomenon. The loaf of sliced bread that I take from the supermarket shelf does not concretely recall and reveal to me a wheatfield, a harvest, a miller, an oven, a hand that blesses and cuts the bread. My gaze is arrested at the surface of the color and texture of the loaf. I know that there is some sort of technical substructure to this opaqueness, presumably some agribusiness in the wheat belt and an automated bakery in the metropolis. But my grasp of this machinery is as vague as my knowledge of its existence. Similarly the pleasant sexual experience that I may have of a human being, either from a glossy page, a television or computer screen, or a singles bar fails to disclose a person in his or her growth, struggles, and aspirations. But in circumstances where I am surrounded by shallow commodities, I tend to become shallow as well. Commodities do not just obviate the exercise of my more profound mental and physical capacities; they actually repel them; my best capabilities must atrophy, and my life will be terribly diminished.

Labor of course places demands on my attention, discipline, and fortitude. But in the divided and degraded labor that is typical of technology, these demands have a draining and impoverishing effect also, though they do not have the pleasant and diverting character that colors leisure. Even on the genuinely demanding and exciting labor at the frontiers of science and industry there lies a shadow of doubt and reproach since the fruits of those endeavors largely lead to the reduction and degradation of work elsewhere and to frequently mindless and frivolous consumption. Let us provisionally agree that a radical theology of technology must be alive to these debilities and follow them up to discover and determine their pattern, extent, depth, and consequences. What might emerge from such work is the insight that the technological style of life does have as an intrinsic feature the incapacity for salvation, i.e., for the wholeness of life. But the decisive mark of human frailty is no longer, as in the pretechnological setting, manifest at the material level as hunger, nakedness, or sickness. Instead, it has become a crippling of our most profound capabilities and consequently a deprivation of things in their own right and depth. To be saved, accordingly, may involve the recovery of one's capacity for the fullness of nature, of art, and for the pretechnological things and practices of daily life that lie half-buried under the surfeit of consumption.

But do such reflections not accomplish too much and too little at the same time? Too much, it seems, because such salvation can be articulated and attained in entirely secular and naturalistic ways as demonstrated by the work of poets and environmentalists such as Wendell Berry and Gary Snyder. Too little, one might think, because they fail to establish the unique and supreme rank of the Christian message. These difficulties are at once plausible and unanswerable. The task is not to find answers to them, but to dispel their appearance of plausibility. These difficulties arise, I believe, from the metaphysical framework whose final elaboration we witness in technology. We must therefore try to penetrate further and pass through the debility that is intrinsic to technology.

To do this let us look more incisively at phenomena we have examined before, and let us consider the immediate source of the technological safety, ease, and comfort that have diminished our capacity for wholeness and the depth of the world. Technology advances and is sustained by regardless power. We exercise such power when we act on the basis of scientific insight by way of engineering or organization in order to procure a result regardless of the recalcitrance or variety of circumstances. This power is manifest in different styles and settings. It is enacted heroically and creatively by the scientist who finds the cure for a disease, by the engineer who develops a new kind of computer memory, by the industrialist who establishes a revolutionary method of production. But since we are all the benefactors and beneficiaries of these enterprises we wield regardless power in a derivative and everyday way. Switches, keys, pointers, buttons, and dials are the insignia of this inconspicuous and consequential power through which we summon up, regardless of time, place, skill, or strength, whatever we need or desire.

In addition to the normal and often inevitable use of regardless power, there is a fugitive recourse to it when we try to escape from the drabness or boredom of our circumstances by imagining ourselves to be in unchallenged possession of an exotic and exhilarating experience beyond the present power of technology. In such flights of fancy we give evidence of how deeply we have assimilated regardless power into our lives. The same evidence is manifest in the resentment or anger we feel when confronted by a problem that will not yield to regardless power, an addiction of some sort or the irritation of a difficult personal relationship. We are scandalized, as indicated earlier, because there is a challenge to what we have come to think of as an irresistible and unquestionable authority.

Such a challenge may humiliate us, but it will not normally unsettle our convictions. We have answered leprosy with antibiotics and disputes about music with earphones. Why should we not hold out for similar answers to alcoholism and jealousy?[8] The upsetting challenges to the rule of regardless power come to us quietly and surprisingly. They can come about in an encounter with nature. Looking at a tree or walking through a meadow, I feel my regardless sovereignty fall away. I am disarmed without being offended and humbled without being humiliated. On the contrary, I am restored to a more profound engagement with the world. Nature is present in its own right and beckons me to respond in the fullness and oneness of my bodily and spiritual faculties. To respond to nature is to acknowledge it and let it be. To be equal to nature and to be careful of it is to experience another and more profound sort of power, one I will call careful power.

Looking back from an experience of careful power at our attempts to settle a personal difficulty in a way that will be secure regardless of human frailty or spontaneity, we can see that success in those terms is a deeper failure in disguise. If through superior technological power I am able to force my will on my opponents regardless of their protests, the consequent arrangement rests on an inevitable residue of resentment, on a hidden source of contamination that may destroy the present order. If my opponents are equals more or less and I deal with them through a technique of domination and manipulation, I have lost them as persons in the fullness of their being. Just as importantly, in accomplishing such pleasant and efficient relationships, I have been an accomplice in the atrophy of my own deepest capacities. This is, of course, the normal event; it has the sanction of the established order and is successful by its standards. But its debility becomes apparent when out of the normal arrangements, be they contentious or comfortable, someone rises to affirm my condition more fully in an act of generosity and goodwill. Restriction and reduction give way, and I am allowed to be fully the one I have wanted to be. There may even come a time when I feel myself empowered to reach out to someone else, and to break through the confinements of those goals, plans, and techniques with which I have tried to bend that person to my will.

But these moments of illumination are overshadowed by ambiguity. Generosity is likely to be overtaken by technology. One is tempted to affirm another's existence by the prevailing standards, to shower that person with the blessings of consumption or to encourage him or her in the very pursuit of the regardless power whose reign was to be overcome in a gesture of care. There are similar problems when we experience and exercise careful power in the midst of nature. We are filled

89

with enthusiasm by the splendor of the wilderness, but the voice of nature becomes faint in the midst of attempts to capture that voice with snapshots of mountains or video-recorded waterfalls. More often than not its call fails to raise us from the comfort of consumption or the applause we earn in the renewed pursuit of technological power when we return to the quotidianity of modern life refreshed by our momentary respite.

There are then episodes where we know ourselves to be channels or recipients of careful power. But they are episodes; careful power makes its entrance on the technological stage and disappears again. As often as not we find ourselves unable to do what in our best moments we know we want to do. St. Paul speaks for us all when he writes, "For I do not do the good I want, but the evil I do not want is what I do" (Rom. 7:19). Careful power is threatened by hopelessness.

Christians are those, I believe, who are encouraged ever and again by Christ; they have been touched by his care and power and so feel empowered in turn. In this way they are able to see and to enact in the episodes of careful power a way of life. Moreover they are convinced by the deeds of Christ to accept his word against their faintheartedness that careful power will prevail over hostility and regardlessness. Christians, of course, do not come to these convictions as the inevitable conclusions of a critique of the technological culture. From their point of view the line of argument presented in these reflections runs backward. Most of them have always and already been touched by the power of Christ, and it is from the responsibility of such power, I believe, that a helpful theological critique of technology may originate.

What has been suggested here is, no doubt, in many ways and for many reasons obscure and ambiguous. Some of the reasons are prosaic; others, I think, are profound. In the latter case it is not a matter of disposing of those reasons but of understanding and accepting them. This is best attempted by meeting the problem of inconclusiveness directly and by asking what definitive evidence there might be for the superiority of careful over regardless power and, more particularly, what evidence for the claim that careful power finds its source in Christ and its appropriate exercise in a world of engaging things. Clearly there is no cogent evidence. But before we surrender to satisfaction or despair we should ask why this is the case.

It helps to draw on common experiences in which one is entirely certain of the existence of some power and yet unable to testify to that fact at all times, regardless of the circumstances. Say I have been touched by the majesty of the wilderness or the force of Bach's orchestral suites. In a calm and thoughtful setting I will speak freely and perhaps effectively of what has moved me. I will trace and highlight the crucial features of these phenomena and recount their eloquence. This can be done when my listeners and I are within hailing distance of nature and within earshot of music in the quiet repose of friendship and inquiry. In such a situation I may be able to draw the listeners into the very presence of these forces and have them see, listen, and agree for themselves. But there are contentious situations where I would not begin to try and make a case for the wilderness or for Bach. These hopeless instances are of several kinds.

There may be a situation of lighthearted sarcasm where someone dares me to protest my devotion to the wilderness. Irreconcilable convictions may clash in a setting of anger and frustration. And philosophers are at times issued the challenge to defend their ultimate concern as one may defend the mind-body identity thesis.

Such settings are immune or deleterious to the kind of discourse that is appropriate to nature and music. In one sense they are hopeless, but not in another. One is not unsettled in one's gratitude to the mountains and to music, and one remains hopeful that on another day the discourse of contention will yield to the discourse of inquiry and testimony. This is an insight that comes slowly especially to young people. Youthful defenders of nature often come to philosophy with a request for a cogent mode of discourse to make their cause prevail regardless of opposition. And as the unwarranted optimism of the pessimists shows, Christians too reach for cogency in argument. When environmentalists are told that such irresistible argumentation is impossible, they are distressed. One must then go on to exhibit how cogent discourse, like regardless power, has its proper sphere; outside those bounds, however, it is not only impossible but undesirable and finally detrimental. To put the point in the words of the foregoing reflections: speaking with regardless force, if it can be done, is to betray and to distort the nature of careful power. The speaking occludes what needs to be conveyed through testimony.

This insight is not new, least of all to Christians. It is at the heart of the tradition to which we feel most indebted.[9] Technology, however, represents the most profound and most concealed threat to this insight, and once we have passed through technology, it gives that insight a new radiance. The thoughtful experience of technology sheds new light on traditional questions. It lets us see in a new or an older way how com-

91

plex the phenomenon of power is. If it is true that the authority of regardless power is dubious or limited, it becomes questionable whether we can ascribe it to God at all. And if we cannot, certain theological views and problems that imply that God possesses regardless power may then no longer be sensible; or, at any rate, they must be rethought from the ground up. Creation and theodicy are among these issues. Omnipotence takes on a new meaning and loses some of the contradictions attendant on its modern technological interpretation. Again, if it is true that the heart of Christianity should inform more profoundly and consequentially than we normally allow the claims we can make on its behalf, new perspectives open up on such issues as Christian dogma and ecumenism. These topics of course extend beyond the confines of the present chapter. Moreover, the antecedents of my conditionals may be false. In conclusion, then, let me turn once more to the question of what kind of force careful power and discourse can have.

It will appear to many that to foreswear cogent argument is to abandon objectivity, and that the parlance of careful discourse may be no more than a cover for subjectivity and arbitrariness. The truth of Christianity would then be definitively hidden or lost. Modern subjectivity is the residue of human nature that seems to remain after the medieval edifice of nature has crumbled or dissolved. Human nature was substantial when it had its rank and mooring in the hierarchy of nature. Once the latter is lost, the former becomes attenuated to a dimensionless if central point. This historical process has induced various types of vertigo, anger at subjective homelessness, intoxication with a novel freedom, endeavors at making the subject the transcendental pivot of a new fundamental theology. What all of such reactions have in common is the belief that technology is nothing more than the most powerful practical agent in the dissolution of the traditional contours of reality and in the procurement of radically new and endlessly open possibilities. The openness and limitlessness of technology in turn confine the subject ever more strictly to its subjectivity.

So rigorously reduced a subject is next to nothing, and as a court of last appeal it must sanction everything. Thus the specter of radical arbitrariness arises together with the modern concept of the subject. Christians naturally see in this undisciplined freedom a radical denial of their tradition, and they are at pains to combat arbitrariness, be it on the basis of a transcendentally redeemed subject or a fundamentalist rejection of modernity and subjectivity. And from the standpoint of apprehension about arbitrariness, the abandonment of regardless power may seem foolish. But in fact the arbitrary liberty that worries so many does not exist, and the attempts to meet it work into the hands of the real problem that lies concealed beneath the semblance of arbitrary subjectivity. Both the mistaking of subjectivity and the misguided endeavor to exorcise arbitrariness spring from a failure to recognize technology for what it is. Technology is not radically liberating at all. Instead, it is an ever more definite template of reality. And the human condition is correspondingly ever more tightly patterned. Subjectivity is just the tinsel packaging for this pattern. The common appeal to the radical freedom of the subject that we encounter daily in many guises is never the battle cry of a truly arbitrary act, far less of a radically new and creative achievement. It is simply the refusal to justify or even to explain an action whose character, by the standards of technology, is all too obvious and conventional.

Thus it is a mistake to believe that the subject subsists in pure integrity or perilous liberty while science and technology are busying themselves in a presumably penultimate way with the elucidation and transformation of the material world. This, to be sure, is not simply an oversight, but part of a destiny that intertwines the occlusion with what is occluded. Yet the concealment is now lifting, I believe, and we can begin to see that the subject was always and already the accomplice of a definite development, i.e., of technology. The call for cogency comes out of this complicity. It is the attempt to cure one's uneasiness with technology by standards of technological efficiency.

Once we begin to see through technology, two points come into focus. The escape from technology by way of cogency is only to fall prey to technology at another level. The passage through technology, on the other hand, opens up a realm of concreteness and simplicity. Since technology is more definite, more limiting, and closer at hand than we have thought, it also discloses a more determinate and forceful alternative than we had dared to hope. That alternative is the world of simple things and practices; this is now the realm of the holy. It is not necessarily the realm of salvation—no arrangement of our practical affairs can by itself effect salvation. Misery and despair, we know, come to pass in the world of engaging things. But such dolor, it seems to me, is still more wholesome than the indolence to suffering and salvation that grows in technology.

Nor is the realm of the holy, as was said before, a stage that Christians finally reach, having gone through various phases of critique and elimination. Rather, because they are Christians, they have always and already resided in that realm albeit unknowingly or diffidently. If the time has now come to accept more fully what all along has been ours, it is still true that for a long time to come technology will constitute the common rule of life. The Christian reaction to that rule should not be rejection but restraint. Technology ought to be revoked as the dominant way of taking up with the world and relegated to securing the margins and underpinnings of our lives. Within that environment we must make a clearing for the celebration of the Word of God. But since technology as a way of life is so pervasive, so well entrenched, and so concealed in its quotidianity, Christians must meet the rule of technology with a deliberate and regular counterpractice.

Therefore a radical theology of technology must finally become a practical theology, one that first makes room and then makes way for a Christian practice. Here we must consider again the ancient senses of theology, the senses that extend from reflection to prayer. We must also recover the ascetic tradition of practice and discipline and ask how the ascesis of being still and solitary in meditation is related to the practice of being communally engaged in the breaking of the bread. The passage through technology discloses a new or an ancient splendor in ascesis. There is no duress or denial in ascetic Christianity. On the contrary, liberating us from the indolence and shallowness of technology, it opens to us the festive engagement with life.

Those of us who take this positive view of life are sometimes brought up short by zealous advocates of the poor, and we may be unsure of how to react, whether with crestfallen political correctnesss or with the angry reminder that the poor will always be with us, but the joy of Christ is not. Perhaps there is a third reply beyond obsequiousness and anger.

6

Liberty, Festivity, and Poverty

In the exploration of the slippery and treacherous region where Christianity and technology have their confluence, Harvey Cox has been a pioneer.[1] His inquiries have met the crucial requirement of insight—they have affirmed certain features that distinguish our time from all others. In this way, his examinations have responded to two present facts that seem obvious and yet are noteworthy. The first is that in the great variety of social and cultural conditions around the globe, those of the advanced industrial countries are most typical, that this is where the modern cultural center of gravity is to be found. The second is closely connected to the first, and the connection can be found in the notion of the typical. The latter is not just the normal and prevalent. As the original word *typos* suggests, the typical bears the imprint of the ideal and most admired standard of today. It is a fact that what is typical and distinctive of our time daily engages the efforts and dedication or at least the desire of a great majority of people. That this profound allegiance to the *typos* of our time should be a massive and total mistake seems incredible to me. There must be something appropriate in this commitment whatever its excesses and liabilities. And a responsible examination of our time must be able to identify and affirm this element of soundness in today's popular orientation. To do so was clearly Cox's intention. But there was a particular attraction to Cox's affirmation, one that it shares with Robert Pirsig's book of some ten years later—*Zen and the Art of Motorcycle Maintenance*.[2] It was the promise to reveal, at the heart of the contemporary *typos*, the fulfillment of a deeply traditional conviction. In Pirsig it is the tradition of contemplative peace of mind, in Cox it is Christianity.

If the first requirement of insight is the recognition of technology as an ideal type, the second requirement that a critique of our culture must meet regards its form. The affirmative spirit must issue, in a fresh terminology, a freshness that expresses the openness and generosity of the inquiring attitude. At the same time the terminology must be careful and confident if it is to carry conviction. Here too Cox proceeds in a gifted and happy way. The very title of his first book is pregnant. It conveys the two movements that Cox thinks to be crucial to the modern period, i.e., secularization and urbanization. Secularization is said to exhibit a trinity of connected dimensions—disenchantment, desacralization, and deconsecration. The result or perhaps the telos of this process, the secular city, has a certain shape and a certain style, the shape having the features of anonymity and mobility, the style consisting of pragmatism and profanity. These are all seen as positive characteristics. To construe anonymity, profanity, and later the separation of work and residence and the organization principle as positive phenomena is to extend a challenge and a promise of redemption to our normal and uncertain views.[3]

The affirmative and inquiring spirit of a contemporary critique must finally have concrete content. It must reach through its terminology the tangible events of our world. It must illuminate the implements, structures, people, and places that we are daily involved with and that constitute the arena and participants of our immediate struggles and hopes. In this regard, Cox shows at least the appropriate intentions though the execution is perfunctory. Cox proposes to examine the switchboard as the image or symbol of anonymity and the highway cloverleaf as the one of mobility.[4] He discusses John Kennedy as a representative of pragmatism and Albert Camus as one of profanity. He illustrates the emergence and variety of the secular city in sketching the salient features of New Delhi, Rome, Prague, and Boston.

Although Cox's *Secular City* is exemplary in meeting conditions that are needed in a helpful critique of our time, what matters decisively is the question whether Cox's analysis is sufficient. Where does his examination finally come to rest? The full title on the book's cover gives an indication. It says: *The Secular City: A Celebration of Its Liberties and an Invitation to Its Discipline.* Liberty and how to extend and secure it are the concerns of Cox's book. What is its guiding notion of liberty? Liberty is understood as disburdenment, disburdenment from the tyranny of nature, of politics, and of values. In its substance, Cox's book is implicitly a reprise of the Enlightenment with two distinctive features.[5] The first is agreeable and consists in the emphasis that Cox places on the continuity between the intellectual and tangible manifestations of liberation. The breaking, e.g., of constraining or oppressive principles of political or social organization comes to be realized in the openness and flexibility of the telephone and transportation systems. More generally, tangible technology is for Cox the essentially beneficial expression of modern freedom. Putting the point more abstractly still, Cox is guided by a unified and trenchant concept of culture where values are seen to be realized unequivocally in the inconspicuous items of daily life, which are all too often taken for granted and ignored.

Whether the character of this continuity is appropriately grasped is another question, one that becomes pressing in the second distinctive trait of Cox's representation of the Enlightenment. Cox sees modern liberation as predominantly the achievement and culmination of the Judeo-Christian tradition. He presses this view to the point where the Enlightenment as a historical and consequential event is entirely overlooked. Before I turn to the real force of this view, I want to note the effect it had on professional theology and organized Christianity. Cox's examination of contemporary culture in its larger extent showed how marginal Christian churches and Christian theology had become to it. The churches had drifted into a safe and secluded haven of traditional practices, cut off from vital experiences and problems. Theology was similarly occupied with arcane and innocuous scholarship. Cox presented a salutary and widely acknowledged challenge to theology, the kind of challenge that is still to be mounted and felt in philosophy.

Regarding the substance of Cox's distinctive view of modern culture and Christianity, one might at first think that pointing out the close kinship if not the identity of Coxian Christianity and secularization on the one side and the tradition and enactment of the Enlightenment on the other is to make a devastating point. If truly modern Christians, atheistic humanists, and the best and the brightest of technologists all have the same goals and policies, is it not more appropriate to speak of the end of Christianity than of its fulfillment in typical contemporary culture? There is, to be sure, within Christianity a long-established tendency to think that a claim to unique supremacy is inseparable from genuine Christianity: *nulla salus extra ecclesiam;* there is no salvation outside of the Christian church. The force of that claim is pressed most in matters of doctrine and not of practices. In this spirit, one could object to Cox's position that merely to look at the practices and practical goals of a society is insufficient to determine whether social endeavors are explicitly derived from Christian doctrine and officially sanctioned by it. They certainly are not in the secular city.

But surely this is a zealous and doctrinaire position. And yet Christians appear to be caught in an unhappy dilemma here. On the one hand it is picayune to insist that people not only be good, but that they should be so for definite and at times arcane theological reasons and from a sense of particular institutional obedience. On the other hand, if as Christians we embrace and affirm good practice in its own right, has not Christianity been reduced to an inconsequential superstructure? The problem can only be resolved, I believe, if we are able to engage in a kind of thinking that gives us a new approach to the distinction between theory and practice.

Accordingly we should weigh Cox's analysis of the secular city by asking where his conception of liberty, whatever its origin, will take us in our daily lives. It takes us out of captivity and oppression and through divisiveness and inequality; but it does not take us anywhere in particular. One can put the point in the familiar language of negative and positive freedom and say that Cox's liberties carry conviction as liberation-from but are entirely dependent for their force on the evils they seek to overcome. Negative liberty becomes silent and timid at the very point where liberation-from needs its final warrant in the proclamation what we are to be free for or to.

But is this a telling complaint? Does not Cox's understanding of freedom share this negative orientation with traditional Christianity? Have not the works and counsels of Christ and his followers always been directed to the liberation from hunger, nakedness, illness, imprisonment, and finally death? And to the extent that there has been a promise of a kingdom to come, has it not always and also been characterized negatively, as an unknowable and ineffable state or event? The answer to these questions must be roughly affirmative, but such an answer would cover up a profound ambiguity in the concept of liberation. Liberation in the secular city differs importantly from what it was in premodern times. Take, for example, liberation from immobility. In the secular city, the cloverleaf of the expressway system is the image of mobility. "Other images of the city," Cox says, "include the airport control tower, high-speed elevators, and perpetually moving escalators in department stores and offices."[6] Of course, these are merely the images and implements of a more important kind of mobility, namely, social mobility. Cox considers particularly residential and occupational mobility. And he sees in them forces that promote social justice, personal growth, and the welfare of society. What about liberation from immobility in a premodern setting? Christ and the Apostles promoted mobility too, one might say. There are several mentions in the Gospels of the lame being healed. And surely such healing promoted greater justice and personal growth. The lame, for instance, were not permitted to be priests according to Leviticus (21:17–20). So where does the difference lie?

To begin with the secular city, the first images of mobility are technological devices. They procure mobility as something that is unquestionably available. A well-designed highway system will allow me to move anywhere at any time in a speedy, safe, and comfortable manner. It is of course no guarantee of higher, i.e., social mobility. But the latter too is secured, if at all, through devices of sorts: civil rights legislation, equal opportunity requirements, quota systems, and the like. Thus liberation is effected by a certain kind of machinery, and liberty becomes a uniform and guaranteed state, i.e., an enduring and reliable situation of disburdenment. The achievement of liberty occurs once and for all as a technological or political breakthrough, as a one-time human accomplishment that becomes effective and permanent in a mechanical or legal device. If the device is well engineered, it will henceforth carry the burden of freedom so that we human beings are now and forever the unencumbered possessors of opportunities. The question of how or even whether we seize these opportunities is no longer part of freedom.

In the Gospels, to the contrary, freedom is not divided into the machinery of liberation and the state of liberty; it always occurs as an event in which liberty and liberation are one, and not once and for all but then and there. Liberty is not a state that allows one to do this or that or nothing at all; it is the active celebration of human wholeness that has been received and appropriated in the event of liberation. "Wilt thou be made whole?" Christ asks the lame man in the King James Version of John (5:6). And in the Acts of the Apostles, when Peter had healed a lame man, it says (3:8): "And he leaping up stood, and walked, and entered with them into the temple, walking, and leaping, and praising God." To be sure, such an event issues in a state too, one of blessedness. But as the further context of these passages shows, it is not a uniformly and reliably enduring state, but one that must ever and again be reaffirmed in the face of human frailty. What endures is the original empowering promise of affirmation.

Let me add three subsidiary points to the issue here at stake. First, it can be summarized this way. Cox is right in stressing that the secular city is promoting mobility, that it mobilizes technical resources to increase and secure people's ability to move hither and yon. Christianity, however, is not concerned with mobility but with movement, the festive movement of the fullness of life. Second, one might object to this argument that it erects a large claim on a very slender exegetical fundament. And that is certainly true. But I believe that a broader exegesis of the Gospels would support that claim. And the view of Christianity as essentially eventful can be uncovered in the Middle Ages as well though with a complexion of its own. The significance of such investigations lies, at any rate, in the light they shed on Christianity today. And that crucial concern will occupy us again later on. Finally, one must ask whether Cox is not aware of biblical movement or mobility. In fact, Cox considers it explicitly and finds that homelessness and mobility, the refusal to restrict divinity to a particular place, thing, or social order, is characteristic of the Hebrew Scriptures and the Gospels.[7] This may well be so. But the ambiguity of mobility would even here cover up the crucial difference between biblical movement and modern mobility.

I now turn briefly to a second stage of Cox's work, which is evident in *The Feast of Fools* of 1969. We might construe the transition this way. Even without the counterpart of the Gospels' eventual and joyful freedom, it would be evident that the liberties celebrated in *The Secular City* are inconclusive and penultimate, that these opportunities require the validation of a central and final enactment. The latter surely comes to pass in festivity and celebration.[8] In the spirit of this construal, Cox rightly sees a movement of progression in his thought. But there is just as certainly a critical turn from *The Secular City* to *The Feast of Fools*. For the progression from technological possibilities to festive actuality has actually failed to occur in typical contemporary life. And therefore a consideration of practices of celebration today must inspire distress and rebuke. This initial tendency is still stronger when Cox considers the fate of fools and of the gift of fantasy that they possess. The fools are the nonconformists who in their words and deeds question the authority of the status quo and who through fantasy dare to conceive of an alternative state of affairs. Such fantastic foolishness is languishing as much in our society as celebration. Thus the book has a strong critical tendency. But so did *The Secular City*. The object of criticism, however, has changed.

In *The Secular City*, the critique was directed toward those political and religious forces that stood in the way of the new, of secularization and urbanization. And the cause that was championed, the new, was seen to be rising powerfully. Speaking on behalf of the clearly ascending culture, *The Secular City* exhibited an affirmative and confident attitude. In *The Feast of Fools* the new, the present culture, is beginning to show troubling deficiencies. "It has produced," Cox says, "too many pedestrian personalities whose capacity for vision and ecstasy is sadly crippled. It has resulted in a deformed man whose sense of a mysterious origin and cosmic destiny has nearly disappeared."[9] And yet Cox remains determined to look for redemption at the leading edge of the secular culture. So he finds a new promise and practice of celebration among the flower children of the sixties and new revolutionary energy among the young militants of the left.

If today we ask whether Cox had indeed discovered the first seedlings of a new festivity and political fantasy, we must certainly answer no. The hippie culture has had a surprisingly wide influence on the habits of dress, sex, eating, and drug use of middle America. But I am not sure that this influence was any more radical than the spread of Japanese goods in the American economy. As regards the force of the militant New Left, it has entirely vanished and been submerged by conservative forces. Cox, I believe, cannot be faulted for his sense of what needed exploration in the late sixties. The phenomenon of festivity was a fitting counterpoint for a critique of that cultural barrenness. Nor should one complain in hindsight that Cox was mistaken in his view of promising developments.

Still, is it possible to learn something from the honorable failure of *The Feast of Fools?* In retrospect, it seems to me, we can see three problems. The first was the joining, however elegant, of festivity and foolish fantasy. The critical denominator that the two issues had in common was too large. It came to saying that the present culture had become overly rigid. And although this common perspective disclosed varied and interesting aspects of our situation, it turned out to be too broad and lacking in trenchancy. And second, without an incisive analysis, the mortal danger of our time remained concealed, and what dangers appeared seemed to be amenable to counterforces that turned out to be innocuous.

The third problem that is left to us by *The Feast of Fools* concerns the force of Christianity in Cox's inquiry. Christianity is the ever-present concern of the book. It becomes most explicit as a theological problem, i.e., in the discussion of radical theology and the theology of hope and in the call for a theology of juxtaposition, one that would allow for both a serious concern with the present and a joyful looking forward to the salvation to come. As regards Christian practice, there are considerations of hopeful trends of celebration and lightheartedness.[10] But the source of hope in these instances is contemporary developments that hold a promise to revive Christianity. Christian practice itself seems more in need of hope than a source of good news. Thus the theology of *The Feast of Fools* assumes hegemony over Christian practice. Here the disquieting and unsettled question of how Christian theory and practice are related arises once more. Summarizing these three problems, we can say that *The Feast of Fools* is clear-sighted and helpful in exposing the typical debility of advanced contemporary culture and in pointing to festive celebration as the orienting center that needs to be recovered. But the critical force of the book is scattered, and the original festivity of Christianity remains at the periphery.

Cox's *Religion in the Secular City* is the book of a turning point, first in the sense that it proclaims the return of religion to the secular city where, so it had seemed to Cox and many others, it was about to be extinguished for better rather than worse. Both that earlier semblance of extinction and the recently proclaimed resurgence of religion stem from a superficial reading of the secular character, I believe. The interaction of technology and religion is steadier than that. And so the overt turning point of Cox's book does not seem epochal to me. Yet there is, in the orientation of the book, an important turn that makes this the most important contribution of Cox's. There is a change in procedure and one of focus, and the two are consonant. In the approach there is a selfless listening to the voices of Christianity, a subordination of theory to practice. The earlier method would rush upon a problematic area, plant three conceptual stakes, then establish a few large claims and hurry on. It has now yielded to a more patient and reflective consideration of the ways in which Christians today struggle to hear and to act on the Word of God. This struggle, rather than its overcoming through liberty or in festivity, is the central concern of the book. Thus it is a more radical book than the preceding two since it considers the basic human condition that makes us capable and needful of salvation.

Let me restrict the discussion to what Cox finds to be crucial in the human condition for a profound and fruitful reception of the Christian message—poverty. Cox's argument goes from the Gospels to the modern situation. In the Gospels, salvation is a promise that is first and most of all extended to the poor. With this I agree. Now the church has forgotten that truth and accommodated itself to the rich and the powerful, so Cox continues. To become vital again, the church must return to the poor. And it has done so most decidedly in the grass-roots communities of Latin America and in the liberation theology that ponders and promotes the work of these communities. Because these currents spring from the vital center of Christianity, Cox concludes, they carry the greatest promise for the revival of Christianity in the secular city. I see great problems in this second part of Cox's argument. Let me try to unfold them by developing observations earlier made about liberty.

Biblical poverty, just like biblical liberty, has a unified depth. This unity has been divided into separate layers through modern science and technology. In the Gospels, poverty is the manifestation of human frailty. In poverty it is apparent that humans cannot through a sheer act of the will, through an effort that would owe nothing to anyone, secure their welfare. In the biblical context and in most premodern settings, material deprivation, disease, and mutilation are the clearest and ever-present signs of human deficiency. The poor and the sick will rarely pretend that they are the masters of their condition. And so they are open to the promise of wholeness, which is fulfilled in healing and the sharing of food. But the attainment of wholeness is more than the mere satisfaction of physiological needs. It is the celebration of life in the spirit of affection and generosity from which salvation issued to begin with. The sick are not just healed; their sins are forgiven; they are freed of hostility and despair, i.e., of their helpless efforts to master their deficiency.

The fullness of life which is the biblical answer to poverty comes into relief against the situation of the rich. They are favored with food and physical health and seem to possess and control the conditions of their wholeness. But precisely their belief in self-sufficient security secludes them from real life, which is celebrated in gratitude and sharing, in the gladly accepted dependence on others, and in the willingness to have others take part in one's gifts. Therefore it is difficult for the rich to be saved. They must, against their wealth, recognize their fundamental frailty and so become poor.

Now in a modern technological setting, poverty as material deprivation and physical suffering is no longer a frequent human condition.

103

More important, poverty in this sense has not been eliminated through extraordinary generosity but through the construction of a highly productive economic machinery. Thus if there is still some kind of typical and fundamental poverty in the technological society, that poverty cannot have biblical character, i.e., its essential shape cannot find its clearest and most eloquent expression in hunger or sickness. Let us assume for the moment that there is a concealed poverty in the technologically affluent countries. I will call it *advanced poverty*.

But there still is, of course, an abundance of starvation and disease outside of the advanced industrial countries. Has it retained its biblical depth and significance? It surely has in individual and concrete circumstances. It still provides an occasion for a healing and sharing in which the joy and radiance of life come to be celebrated. But in a general and political sense, the misery of the developing countries has lost its biblical profoundness too. And it has done so in symmetry with the disappearance of biblical poverty in the advanced countries. In light of technological affluence, global misery is no longer an essential sign of human frailty but a scandal, a cruel and unnecessary misfortune since the elimination of that misery is clearly possible, not only conceptually but in fact; for the technological machinery of production could be expanded to satisfy the physical needs of all peoples, and such an expansion would not expose the technologically affluent to material deprivation or even hardships. In this way, global poverty has attained, necessarily, I believe, a bitterness and brutality that make such poverty a difficult and contradictory setting for the promise of salvation. Let us call this kind of condition *brute poverty*.

In the modern period then, biblical poverty has been split into brute poverty and advanced poverty. In the concluding part of this essay I want to claim that although brute poverty in its scandalous starkness has first claim on our practical efforts, it is advanced poverty that requires our reflection and eventually our decisive action. Advanced poverty is the pivotal problem of contemporary Christianity. Regarding brute poverty, then, the question is not whether it deserves our sympathy and dedication. Unquestionably it does. The question is rather whether it constitutes a theologically fruitful and forward-looking situation. Cox thinks so because brute poverty is such a radical challenge to us both as Christians and as members of the technological culture. The poor of the developing countries have a right to be helped. And the refusal of the rich societies to provide help constitutes oppression or at least culpable callousness. Hence one can well say that brute poverty is the result of oppression.[11] But poverty seen in the framework of rights is no longer or not yet a final religious issue. The violation of a right must certainly be objectionable from a religious point of view. But to honor a right is a religiously inconclusive act since rights in the modern era are morally minimal though fundamental entitlements. Thus to demand of others that they honor a right and nothing more is not to confront them fully in a religious sense. To speak of poverty as always being the result of oppression by the powerful is to move poverty into a quasi-legal framework and away from the center of religious concern.

This is not to excuse the callous and the oppressors. It is to say that Cox accepts a religiously impoverished notion of poverty. That same diminishment is apparent when one looks at the claimants' side of the dispute. Precisely because brute poverty is so brutal and senseless, its elimination will not be the occasion for the rise and celebration of a joyful sense of wholeness. In fact, the normal successor of brute poverty is advanced poverty. No person of good will would want to save people from advanced poverty by keeping them in brute poverty. The latter must be eliminated by all means. But when we consider the force that the appeals from brute poverty have had for a reform of the global distribution of affluence and when we look for a consideration of this problem on Cox's part, we will, as Cox's reviewers have noted, be disappointed and perplexed.[12] It is not that the affluent are uninformed of the bitterness of brute poverty, nor is it the case that the rich, though informed, are economically unable to help. Rather we must assume that they are suffering from an incapacity to be moved by misery. And that incapacity, I want to urge, is a feature of advanced poverty. Thus brute poverty points us to advanced poverty in two ways. First, the religious inconclusiveness of brute poverty and its normal supersession by advanced poverty suggest that if there is today a decisive setting for the advent of the Gospel's good news, it must be advanced poverty. And second, if there is to be any hope for a vigorous and imminent attack on brute poverty, it hinges on our ability to open up in advanced poverty a sense of compassion and a readiness to share.

But so far I have passed over the nature of advanced poverty except to say that it is characteristic of the advanced industrial society and that it exhibits a profound insensitivity to the misery beyond its boundaries. Yet if it is crucial to the typical modern condition, we should find at least traces in Cox's inquiry. We do so in the critique of modernity, particularly where Cox examines a major commercial airport as "modernity incarnate."[13] Whereas in *The Secular City* the airport control tower and the airways had been symbols of modern liberty, the airport now serves as an illustration of the decline and approaching end of the modern era.

To train his observations on our problem, we might say that, as the modern world declines, general impoverishment rises. The general poverty that Cox sees has brute features. There is a decay of competence and efficiency, a rising threat of oppression, conflict, and death.[14] But Cox speaks in an equally critical and distressed tone of another ill in which the troubling features are fused with an appearance of a sleek brilliance and a pleasant affluence. This gleaming comfort is at the same time barren and shallow; there is a lack of untamed life and of intimacy with living things. Cox fittingly concludes that no missionary every faced "as unpromising a field as someone who is sent to make God's ways known here in the Big Airport, the modern world in miniature."[15]

I think if one were to follow such reflections further, one would find that the appeal to brute poverty is a misdirected effort to locate human incompleteness in the midst of technology. Technology is the systematic eradication of profound poverty, and it is just that success that gives rise to advanced poverty. It is the accomplishment of unquestionable comfort and security that has all but paralyzed our capacity to help and to be helped and so to have part in the fullness of life. Advanced poverty, one might say, is a radically aggravated and universalized form of the condition of the rich of which the Bible speaks.

Already in *The Feast of Fools*, Cox had noticed and criticized this peculiar vacuity and superficiality of modern life. But the examination of the contemporary condition in the earlier book was finally too scattered to be helpful. In his later work, Cox is more insistent in his critique and more confident of Christianity as providing a forceful reply to modern debility. But again, it seems to me, the investigation breaks off too soon. The concluding sentence of the quotation above suggests that the impoverishment of life in the most advanced technological setting, what I have called advanced poverty, constitutes a singularly difficult challenge for Christianity. Following fundamentalist apprehensions, Cox had earlier in his book entertained that possibility, but then dismissed and, I think, trivialized it by submerging the modern condition in sweeping cultural and historical vistas.[16] The persistent and unsolved problem in Cox's reflections appears to be this. Cox has shown extraordinary verve in his turn to the concreteness and peculiarity of the modern condition; and there is a steady deepening of insight. But the final and decisive steps are not yet taken.

Accordingly, we are in Cox's debt for his insistence that an understanding of poverty is needed for the revival of Christianity. But we must go forward to a more critical view of poverty and distinguish its biblical, brute, and advanced forms. Let me conclude with some observations of the tasks and consequences of that enterprise. At its center there will have to be a consideration of poverty as a fundamental human condition. I want to suggest two points regarding that consideration, the first pertaining to the force of claims that we can hope to advance on this topic, the second concerning the relation of Christian theory and practice.

To grasp today's poverty fundamentally we must uncover it, as urged before, in the typical circumstances of contemporary life. Here I can add nothing to the positive task beyond the hints already provided. But I want to caution against the tendency of overstating or, really, mistaking what one can hope to discover about poverty. We might say with Karl Rahner that human poverty is "a must in the history of salvation," not something that ought to be this way but will have to be this way.[17] This is to experience and to take human frailty seriously. Such serious attention, however, should not issue in the attempt to furnish an ontological or transcendental proof for the necessary or universal debility of human existence. Not only is such ethical foundationalism doomed to fail in point of theory. More important, it tends to go hand in hand with a soteriological imperialism. Believing to have found an a priori want in humans, one is easily inclined to see in Christianity a correspondingly universal and unsurpassable complement. But the belief that we can secure for ourselves and possess unconditionally valid assurances regarding our basic condition has a fatal kinship with advanced poverty and is too close to it to discern the character of that destitution.

This finally brings us to the problem of Christian theory and practice. The remarks above suggest that a doctrinaire and foundationalist theory is inappropriate to the task of Christianity in the postmodern world. But surely there is a need for reflective theorizing, for a consideration of the force of Christianity in the concrete circumstances of the technological culture. Reflective theory must take its guidance and its principle of tolerance from the history and the immediacy of Christian practice. Practice should be clear and full-bodied in its celebrations but generous and unobtrusive in its doctrines.

But where can we find vigorous Christian practices? We do find them on Sunday mornings, and this should give us hope. During the week, however, the life of a typical Christian hardly differs from that of an agnostic or atheist. What does it take to shake us out of our normalcy and complacency? Catastrophic events? Heroic acts of courage?

7

Courage and Fortitude

We will never forget the terror of September 11, 2001, but neither will we forget the heroic efforts of the firefighters and the police officers who rushed into the World Trade Center to help people escape and who paid for their courage with their lives. The catastrophes of that day, moreover, have led to extraordinary testimonies of sympathy, generosity, and dedication. Beyond heroism and high-mindedness, however, a disquieting question begins to stir: Does it take a disaster to rouse us to virtuous action? Is our ordinary common life hostile or indifferent to moral excellence?

Courage is a fine probe for this difficult problem, and William Miller has written a helpful guide to the enigma of courage.[1] A consideration of this virtue must begin with the puzzles of psychology, for it seems that courage is inexplicably distributed. Some people have it and some don't. But if courage is simply a matter of course for the truly courageous, should we—turning now to ethics—give them moral credit? Are not the fears and terrors we feel in the face of danger the crucial obstacles courage must overcome in order to be courage? If those terrors simply paralyze us, should we not be held blameless? But if we are blameless, what is the meaning of cowardice? Is cowardice the deliberate refusal to confront danger? Yet it has been said that in war most men overcome cowardice because they are not courageous enough to say no to war.

Such questions are more than conundrums of idle reflection. It is a strength of Miller's book that it brings up the particulars of courage and cowardice in reports and testimonies from the ancient Greeks to the Vietnam War. Miller is suspicious of the opinions of philosophers who unduly extol the element of courage closest to their trade—the deliberate assessment of the dangers to be faced. At the same time, it is Aristotle's treatment of courage in the *Nicomachean Ethics* that provides the framework for *The Mystery of Courage*. Miller also adopts Aristotle's view as to the foremost setting of courage—mortal danger in war.

Such glorification offends our sense of justice and peace. Students of ethics, at least since Immanuel Kant, have insisted that moral norms and accomplishments must be open to all, not just to warriors and soldiers and certainly not to only those soldiers who have "the good fortune" of seeing a war. Christians share Kant's inclusiveness. More important, they have been told that the meek, not the courageous, shall inherit the earth.

Being part of virtue ethics, however, courage is closer to Christianity than it is to modern ethics. Modern moral theories typically aspire to principles of universal scope and cogent force, and the Gospels in places read like an explicit rejection of principle ethics. When Jesus is asked for a definition, he tells a story. When in a parable the problem of the impartial administration of justice arises, the particular takes precedence over the universal, and the claims of justice are overruled by the grace of charity.

Virtue ethics has recently had a scholarly renaissance. Virtue ethicists, however, have spent most of their energy on showing that their brand of ethics can equal or surpass in explanatory power what its rivals—Kantian ethics and utilitarianism—have to offer.[2] Besting its competitors, so the argument goes, virtue ethics gives a more holistic view of the moral life; it not only insists on blamelessness but promotes moral excellence; and it recognizes that the vitality of the good life is not codifiable in a set of principles.

Through William Bennett's best-selling *Book of Virtues*, virtue ethics appears to have enjoyed some popular success.[3] But I venture to guess that the *Book* was more often bought and given as a present than lovingly read to one's children. Here too the virtue of courage can serve as a guide, in this case to the circumstances that render recent virtue ethics (Bennett's included) so ineffectively pious. The moral force of courage depends precisely on its circumstances. When you think about it, all virtues are in a crucial sense circumstantial.

Virtues are in important part moral skills, and a skill that is illuminating in one setting, the skill, say, of reading tracks in the Rockies, can be irrelevant in another, e.g., the skill of reading tracks in Chicago's

Loop. Principle ethics, to be sure, was intended to rule anywhere at any time. Recent virtue ethics has allowed itself to be co-opted on this point by its rivals, and as a consequence its teachings seem old-fashioned and without purchase on our predicaments. Translators make some linguistic concessions to modernity, rendering as "self-control" what used to be called "temperance" and using "moral strength" in place of "continence."

Miller shows well that what is courage in hand-to-hand combat is foolishness in meeting a hail of bullets, and is plain stupidity in standing up to mortar shells. He recounts testimony to the effect that one can revel in courage when one engages in a perilous foray while courage inevitably seeps away, except among psychopaths, in the grind and squalor of trench warfare. In fact, Aristotle already had an awful time with courage because its setting had shifted from the heroic to the civic.

Courage was the defining virtue of the Homeric hero, and Aristotle evidently loved heroic courage above all. When in the *Nicomachean Ethics* he says of the virtuous man that "he would prefer an hour of rapture to a long period of mild enjoyment, a year of beautiful life to many years of ordinary existence, one great and glorious exploit to many small successes," he surely had in mind Achilles who lived and died by this precept.[4] And when it comes to defining heroic courage, Aristotle ranks courage according to the dangers the hero meets, mortal danger being the severest test; and he goes on to ask: "What form of death then is a test of courage?" Aristotle answers: "Presumably that which is the most beautiful. Now the most beautiful form of death is death in battle, for it is encountered in the midst of the greatest and most beautiful of dangers."[5]

Aristotle must have been thinking of the grace and athleticism of heroic, warrior-to-warrior combat. Translators invariably mute Aristotle's aesthetic delight in war by translating "beautiful," not unreasonably, as "noble," "fine," "admirable," and the like.[6] In any case, warriors in Aristotle's time no longer fought for glory and spoils but to protect the city, the women, and the children. And there was little beauty, if some nobility, in the famously effective Greek phalanx. The main concern was to keep those heavy shields locked to make an impenetrable wall and to advance steadily and, if possible, irresistibly.[7] Though Aristotle makes no explicit distinction between heroic and civic courage, his sympathies are evident, and he wistfully concludes that civic courage belongs among the lesser kinds of courage although it is first among them "since it most closely resembles true courage."[8]

Like Aristotle, Thomas Aquinas was able to look back to a heroic age when courage was a defining and unequivocally glorious Christian virtue. Persecution in the Roman Empire was the ultimate test of faith, hope, and charity, and to suffer martyrdom was to pass the test triumphantly. But Thomas was just about as far from the time of martyrs as Aristotle was from the time of heroes—about a thousand years. By the thirteenth century, the church was secure and flourishing. To lead a faithful life no longer required a confrontation with torture and death but rather the daily struggle with the hardships and distractions of everyday life.

To agree with Aristotle, whom he simply calls "the Philosopher," was nearly as important to Thomas as being faithful to Christian doctrine. Hence he did not want to deny that war is the preeminent setting of courage, but he widened the meaning of war to include particular attacks on one's life or well-being.[9] Moreover, he divided courage into an aggressive and an enduring component and, appealing to a throwaway line of Aristotle's, he elevated endurance over acts of daring, a point Miller is characteristically loath to accept.[10] He wants to call this attitude *fortitude* and make it a separate virtue.

English is blessed with numerous pairs of near-synonyms that allow one to mark subtle differences in meaning. *Fortitude* certainly is closer to the mental and patient side of encountering dangers well, while courage has a greater affinity to the physical and daring side of confronting perils. Thomas, however, had just one word (it happens to be Latin *fortitudo*) as did Aristotle (Greek *andreia*, whose original meaning was *manliness*). And all this suggests that Thomas's thinking is likely to be more helpful to our predicament than Aristotle's.

Thomas did not complain about the loss of heroic circumstances, but neither did he conceal his admiration for the glory of martyrdom.[11] As Miller tells us, however, David Hume and Adam Smith, who saw the modern refinement of manners and the promise of technological comfort, began to worry about the fate of courage.[12] The dangers and hardships that made courage prosper were receding, but the need for the moral vigor of courage continued.

For more than three hundred years now, modern technology has been dissolving traditional structures and indulging our weaknesses. But every generation, or at least every century, rediscovers these forces and fears for what structures and virtues have been spared so far. Regarding structures, Marx and Engels memorably noted in 1848 already: "All that is solid melts into the air, all that is holy is profaned."[13] But then came

Nietzsche and, in our day, Daniel Bell, Christopher Lasch, and a host of others.

As for courage, Smith's and Hume's apprehensions were followed in 1896 by William James's call for "The Moral Equivalent of War" as a setting where in peaceful times the "military ideals of hardihood and discipline would be wrought into the growing fibre of the people."[14] The details of the process, as James imagined them, strike us today as strange, not to say bizarre, and are worth quoting because they show how intractable the predicament of courage had really become.

> To coal and iron mines, to freight trains, to fishing fleets in December, to dishwashing, clothes-washing, and window-washing, to road-building and tunnel-making, to foundries and stoke-holes, and to the frames of skyscrapers, would our gilded youths be drafted off, according to their choice, to get the childishness knocked out of them, and to come back into society with healthier sympathies and soberer ideas. They would have paid their blood-tax, done their own part in the immemorial human warfare against nature; they would tread the earth more proudly, the women would value them more highly, they would be better fathers and teachers of the following generation.[15]

These words might as well have been written three hundred years ago for all the distance in situation and sentiment that separates us from them. Mining is a declining industry, freight trains have been passed by trucks and planes, steel furnaces have all but disappeared. Most important, we would not think of restricting whatever moral toughening to young men, nor would we confess, much less give praise, to "the immemorial human warfare against nature." We have crossed a cultural divide from the modern to the postmodern era.

Or have we? Consider Miller's lament:

> There has been a recent spate of books and movies that look with great nostalgia on World War II, written by or directed by those who did not fight, who now in their middle age, when it is very safe for them to indulge this kind of wistfulness, think it vaguely amiss that they missed out on war. Most of my social class in the United States (myself included) bought substitutes for the only war we were eligible to fight in and would no doubt do so again. So when in middle age I come at last to believe that a nation builds up a moral treasury of merit by the sacrifices of its people in war and I begin to worry, like those ancient moralists, that we grow fat, lazy, and contemptible amidst our plenty, I don't have a leg to stand on to make that claim. My father could; he fought; but he is too wise to make it.[16]

Is *moral* courage the virtue that remains, now that physical danger and hardship have receded? Not in the way Miller thinks of it, and he has pretty well captured the common sense of it. Moral courage is the willingness to suffer discomfort or disgrace in the defense of what is right and good. Not that the need for such courage has entirely evaporated, nor is physical courage obviated across the board. But in a decent society, there is no need for the regular exercise of moral courage, and the more we succeed in securing justice and fairness through laws and regulations, the less call there is for moral courage. If courage is to be a virtue, however, it must be a habit, a moral skill that is regularly tested and exercised.

A skill is context-specific, and perhaps the real question is not how we can hope to situate a traditional virtue in contemporary circumstances but what circumstances today are most hostile to a Christian life and what sort of moral skill they require. The relevant circumstances can't be those of safety and well-being brought about by public health measures, medical care and insurance companies, wholesome food and clean water, etc. Surely God does not want us to court and suffer preventable harms.

Our morally crucial circumstances are the exact mirror image of those that made for martyrs. Where theirs were overt, ours are concealed; where theirs were mortal to their bodies, ours are lethal to the soul; and where theirs tore them out of their normal life, ours channel our lives within the unquestioned banks of the technological culture: You come home from work, frazzled and spent. You walk into the kitchen and are not surprised that the children have left already and your spouse is not yet home. You find yourself walking to the refrigerator; you take what you like most and put it in the microwave. You stare at the paper on the kitchen table; it's Wednesday, your favorite TV show is on, followed by a game of the home team. Your pulse quickens a little. The show is good, your spouse comes home, you exchange a few words, the game is boring, you move to the den to do an overdue memo on the computer. But first you check your e-mail, the latest news, you happen on the ESPN Web site. They offer you a video game, you play it for a while, your spouse is going to bed. You decide to call it a day.

Has this been an un-Christian evening? You have not coveted your neighbor's spouse, you have not stolen anything, you have not ordered anyone around. What you have done seems unexceptional. There were moments of a pleasant sort of freedom when you were able to eat what you liked at the time you liked, while watching the program you liked.

114

There were moments of mild excitement when you anticipated the game or started to play the video game. Sullenness may have overtaken you in the end, but at least you did not have to presume on anyone's time or attention.

This sort of retreat to a cocoon of autonomy has been spreading enormously in the last generation as Robert Putnam has shown so impressively and depressingly.[17] Yet a life without grace and gratitude is un-Christian, not in this failing or that, but from the ground up. It has become incapable of redemption. This is not an all-or-nothing affair, of course. But the rising specter of irredeemability is stalking all of us. It is, if anything, more hidden in the active phases of the technological culture, when we go shopping, finish the basement, or go after a promotion. There is then more activity, promise, and companionship. Yet all of this is in the service of more consumption, of reviving its charms, and of deepening its hold on us.

Amazingly, the world of personal engagements and engaging things is still right around us, as a close possibility if not as an actual practice. Here on the shelf is the poetry we could read to one another, there in the corner are the flute and the guitar we could play together. Right next to the kitchen is the dining-room table we could gather around. And not far from our home are the playing fields where we could teach our daughter tennis or join a softball league with our beloved. There is the museum where local painters are showing their work and the concert hall where the citizens' symphony plays.

These are the places where patience is tried and generosity rewarded, where disappointments can't be escaped and grace descends in what Virginia Woolf calls moments of being.[18] Those places are the precincts of faith where redemption comes into view again as the perfection the world cries out for.

To social critics the devotion to focal things at home and to communal celebration abroad may seem like pretty weak tea, bland and retrograde goals, better perhaps than consumption at home and shopping in public, but not exactly the stuff of bold designs and revolutionary politics. Nor would the conservative champions of courage get excited. Where are the hardships? Where the risks?

And yet, all we would have to do to become "courageous" again is cross the threshold from the TV den to the dining room or from the home to the realm of communal celebrations. The physical thresholds are in fact low and smooth, but they coincide with moral thresholds that are so high and hard that few of us cross them. Those are the thresholds of unencumbered self-determination, of seductive promises, of self-indulgence, and of freedom from accountability. A residual tradition or the implorations of a loved one can occasionally get us to the other side of comfort, and we feel surprised and grateful. And a calamity like the recent suicide attacks can break and remove the barriers to engagement and solidarity. But the blandishments of technology will not disappear. The decision to cross the thresholds must be made again and must be made daily. Steadiness in crossing them can come only from an arduously acquired and faithfully maintained habit—a virtue, as Aristotle and Aquinas would call it. Courage is not quite the right name for it, but fortitude is. Fortitude needs to become the defining virtue of the postmodern era.

There are, of course, many thresholds to be crossed, and there are as many areas where fortitude can be exercised and rewarded. From a broadly cultural point of view, any kind of regular and skilled engagement with an appropriately demanding and commanding thing will be welcome. Christians should welcome and support such a genuinely and constructively pluralist culture. But since they want to center their lives on the Word of God and the Breaking of the Bread, two cultural practices are of particular importance to them—the culture of the word and the culture of the table.

8 ■

The Culture of the Word and the Culture of the Table

Social theorists tend to find society in a state of crisis more often than in a period of flowering. But in recent years findings of crisis and peril have been especially numerous. More significant still, what has been particularly worrisome to the critics is the health of the middle class. Given the social diversity and economic volatility of the United States, the middle class is not just the middle segment in the hierarchy of status and prosperity, but the steadying and anchoring force of society. The middle class has traditionally provided the power if not always the leadership to keep the excesses of the upper class in check and the miseries of the lower class within bounds. But now this centering force seems itself in danger of attenuation and dislocation.

Already in 1989, Barbara Ehrenreich had published her passionate and provocative study of the perils besetting the middle class and striking it with the *Fear of Falling*.[1] Meanwhile the genteel *New Yorker* has taken pity on the middle class, asking plaintively "Who Killed the Middle Class?" on October 16, 1995, and lamenting that there "Ain't No Middle Class" on December 11, 1995.[2]

But these assessments and plaints are strangely inconclusive. They miss both the appearance and the heart of contemporary culture. To all appearances, American middle-class culture has, at least since the seventies, been tranquil and steady, free of social unrest and material deprivations. In the olden days a crisis was marked by marauding bands, widespread starvation, or lethal epidemics. Nothing even approaching such calamities has lately been seen in our society.

As for the heart of contemporary culture, the social maps that the critics give us have a blank space where one should expect to find the living center of society. The moral and economic critics fear for the stability and prosperity of the social structure but appear to take it for granted that as long as firmness and affluence are secured, the good life will take care of itself and will naturally fill out the framework.

That consumption is at the center of the supposedly good life and casts a shadow of doubt on the actual goodness of our lives is noted occasionally. Barbara Ehrenreich has chronicled the uneasiness that arises when we contemplate our devotion to consumption, and she has well described the mutations that consumption has undergone without ever losing its infectious force.[3] The elusiveness of the cultural center of contemporary society is illustrated by Charles McGrath's attempt to find enlightenment about our cultural state of affairs in a "brand-new genre," one he calls "the prime-time novel"—the weekly network dramatic series.[4] Fifty-four point four million Americans watch them every night, an impressive number when you consider that if 1 percent of them bought and read a copy of the old-style genre novels once a month, we would have a literary revolution on our hands. What McGrath values in these programs is that "they frequently attain a kind of truthfulness, or social seriousness, that movies, in particular, seem to be shying away from these days."[5] What he found

> were stories involving abortion rights and affirmative action; a murder, very similar to a famous Westchester case, in which a young man, suffering an alcoholic blackout, killed two people he mistakenly took to be his parents; and the apprehension and conviction of a Katherine Ann Power-like fugitive.[6]

Is this what typically happens to you or your parents, your neighbors, or your colleagues? Does not the real significance of television lie not so much in *what* people watch as in the fact *that* they watch it so religiously? McGrath does note that the "failure of TV drama to take itself into account is one of the great oddities of the medium."[7] On reflection this does not seem odd at all, for who would want to stare down an infinite regress? A realistic portrayal of television would come to showing a family watching television. And if what *they* are watching is a slice of typical family life it would be another family watching TV—television-watching families watching television-watching families ad infinitum.

The suspicion that there is nothing but an infinite abyss at the heart of American culture has haunted more than a few students of the subject and has made them recoil from the heart of the matter. Journals such as *Material Culture* and *Technology and Culture* cling to safely circumscribed historical phenomena. Norman J. G. Pounds's *Hearth and Home: A History of Material Culture* stops short of the twentieth century.[8] Robert Crunden's *A Brief History of American Culture* sticks to politics and the high, yet inconsequential, culture of literature and the fine arts.[9]

The crisis of contemporary culture is as elusive as the heart of the culture that is ailing. The evidence of trouble that we are presented with is nothing but the symptom of a hidden and chronic malady. One begins to suspect that contemporary culture cannot heal because its injury is so concealed.

To act on this suspicion is the beginning of philosophy. Bringing the malaise of contemporary culture into focus is a philosophical enterprise, and the notion of *culture* is a good vehicle to get the enterprise underway. Culture is something more than and other than politics, economics, or aesthetics. Helpfully it has a descriptive and a normative sense. In the former, as E. B. Tylor put it in 1871, it means "that complex whole which includes knowledge, belief, art, morals, law, custom, and any other capabilities and habits acquired by man as a member of society."[10] At least as old is the notion of culture as an ideal of human flourishing and perfection.

To lift the veil of indistinctness from contemporary culture in the descriptive sense, let us look at it against the background of normative conceptions of culture, the culture of the word and the culture of the table. To begin with the culture of the word, I mean by it practices of conversation and reading. Though such practices have normative status today, they are by no means elitist. They were fully realized in the middle class of the first half of the last century. Consider the testimony of Norman Maclean, author of the celebrated "A River Runs Through It."[11] Here is what he says of his youth in Missoula, Montana:

> After breakfast and again after what was called supper, my father read to us from the Bible or from some religious poet such as Wordsworth; then we knelt by our chairs while my father prayed. My father read beautifully. He avoided the homiletic sing-song most ministers fall into when they look inside the Bible or edge up to poetry, but my father overread poetry a little so that none of us, including him, could miss the music.[12]

119

Young Norman had to do a lot of his own reading as well as writing.[13] But the culture of the word extended beyond writing and literature into his daily life. Here is more testimony:

> But when I was young—certainly no older than 17 or 18—I was telling Montana stories myself. There was a small bunch of us of the same age who would sit in the evening on the steps of the First National Bank in Missoula, then owned by the Jacobs family, and tell Montana stories. We were all young, but we all worked in the woods in the summer, and I don't think you can be a Montana storyteller unless you have worked in the woods or on ranches.[14]

As Maclean's life teaches us, words beget words; the culture of reading and narrating issues in literature.

But obviously the culture of the word has ceased to recreate itself. "I need hardly tell you," Maclean notes sorrowfully, "that families no longer read to each other. I am sure it leaves a sound-gap in family life."[15] Culture, however, abhors a vacuum and has filled the gap with television, or has not rather television insinuated itself into family life and choked off reading? How could that happen?

One way of setting off reading against television is to borrow from information theory and ask, How many bits of information do you need for a minute of reading as opposed to a minute of television? There is no hard-and-fast way to determine this, but 7,000 bits per minute of reading is a defensible answer. On a compact disc, a minute of sound requires about 100 million bits. Video, as we know, is a hog when it comes to bits; so, depending on how compressed, it is a multiple of the 100 million sound bits per minute. In an obvious way, then, video is infinitely richer than a text, and the people who turn from books to television turn from what is austere to what is rich as who would not?

Television is not only richer than reading but, in a different way, richer than storytelling too. If today one feels the need to be entertained by the presentation of a captivating event, one does not have to wait till it is evening and one's friends show up at the First National Bank, nor is one at the mercy of a particular storyteller and the hard and cold steps of the bank. Instead you can at any time summon the dramatic rendering of whatever story and enjoy it in the comfort of your couch. Thus technology not only enriches our lives but also furnishes it with a kind of freedom that differs importantly from the political liberty that normally comes to mind when we talk of freedom. The promise of technology is one of material and social liberty, the promise of disburdenment from the pains and limits of things and the claims and foibles of humans.

Thus the full promise of technology has always been one of a special liberty and prosperity. The promise inaugurated the modern era and has to this day animated our society's most coordinated and strenuous efforts. It comes to the fore in advertisements, the public proclamations of our furtive aspirations. Most every advertisement stages versions of two formulas: "Now you no longer have to . . ."—the promise of liberation—and "Now you can . . ."—the promise of enrichment.

When over 54 million people in this country sit down in the evening to take in one of the "prime-time novels," who is it that is laying such a wealth of spectacles at their feet? Obviously not the remaining 200 million plus Americans the way the troupe of players did for Hamlet and the royal court at Elsinore. Instead contemporary folk are entertained by a complex machinery that touches their private sphere through TV sets, VCRs, and DVD players and extends from there to transmission devices, senders, studios, and scriptwriters and extends laterally to utility grids, manufacturing facilities, and research and development labs.

Technology has delivered liberty and prosperity not through magic as fairy tales have it, nor through servitude as feudal lords enjoyed it, but through increasingly sophisticated and powerful machineries. As their development has progressed, the goods that these machineries are procuring have become available more instantly, ubiquitously, easily, and safely—more commodiously in an older sense of the word. Such goods may well be called commodities, not just because they are commercially available but, more important, because of their comfort and convenience as the word commodity, again in a less common sense, suggests.

Once it is clear how the culture of the word has been replaced by the commodities of entertainment through an elaborate machinery, one can see a like pattern of displacement throughout the culture. The culture of the table, the careful preparation and the daily or festive celebration of meals, has been invaded by the commodious flexibility and variety of foods that are bought ready-made, stored safely and easily, and prepared in an instant.[16] Underlying this commodity are the vast machineries of agriculture, food industry, and supermarkets, and by the ubiquitous machineries of cars, refrigerators, and microwaves. Wherever you turn, whether to matters of transportation, health, the arts, or, increasingly, education, you see the same conjunction of commodification and mechanization having transformed and still transforming our culture.

The pattern of this transformation is well instantiated by any of the technological devices that surround us in daily life. The commodity of a TV set is the smoothly moving, brilliantly colored picture and its contents. The machinery is known to exist somewhere behind the screen, beyond the competence and intelligibility of ordinary people. It can change significantly, say from analog to digital transmission or from cathode-ray tubes to active matrix screens, unbeknownst to the consumer who merely registers an improvement in the size, reliability, resolution, and space requirements of the commodity.

A definite vocable for this cluster of technological phenomena—the cultural displacements, the commodification and mechanization, and their embedding in contemporary culture—is the pattern of the technological device or what I have called the *device paradigm*. And we can now ask, What is the cumulative cultural effect of the device paradigm and who is responsible for that effect? In important part the effect has been most beneficial. There are burdens of hunger, sickness, and confinement that the device paradigm has lifted from the shoulders of the advanced industrial countries, and no responsible person would want those afflictions to return.

This constructive layer in the development of modern technology has always overlaid a more profound feeling of loss and betrayal. But during its most constructive phase, roughly from 1850–1950, technology was mostly seen as a beneficial force. Increasingly, however, the layer of doubt and sorrow has grown, and the benefits of technology have become thinner.

Who is responsible for this development? To speak of the device paradigm or of technology as doing this and preventing that is to imply a premature and tendentious answer to this question. It is to subscribe to technological determinism, the view that technology is a force in its own right, irresistibly forcing our hand as we shape our culture. Though many a critic of technology has lapsed into the determinist position on occasion, it is normally and rightly repudiated. In the prevailing view, technology is an ensemble of neutral structures and procedures that can be used for well or ill—the instrumentalist view of technology.[17]

Instrumentalism no doubt applies to many situations and quandaries in the technological culture. But it deflects attention from the crucially different ways cultural decisions are made in our society. Our daily decisions are for the most part channeled and banked by fundamental decisions that are no longer at issue. Using or not using the interstate highway system is not a matter of choice anymore for most of us, and neither are the moral consequences of long commutes and the neglect of family, neighborhood, and inner city. When we finally come home, late and exhausted, greeted by a well-stocked refrigerator, a preternaturally efficient microwave, and diverting television, there is little choice when we fail to cook a good meal and summon the family to the dinner table.

What the instrumentalist fails to see is that we live in a world that is patterned after the device paradigm, a life where we pay our dues to the machinery of the device through labor and where in our leisure time we surrender to the diversions of commodities. We value work because it is, more so than citizenship or education, the crucial certificate of membership in this society. We value leisure because it is still ringing with the echoes of liberty, prosperity, and self-realization. But we sense at a deeper level that a life divided between labor that is not fulfilling and leisure that is not ennobling is not worth living. We are all implicated in this way of life, and our implication in the device paradigm is a difficult and complex relation. Contrary to what the technological determinists would have us believe, we are not simply and entirely under the sway of technology. And *pace* the instrumentalists, we are not normally elevated above technology as wakeful and rational choosers.

Our implication in the device paradigm of technology, I believe, is at the heart of the crisis of contemporary culture. This implication, often shading over into complicity, accounts for the sporadic sorrow we feel at the loss of cherished things and practices that were part of an older culture, now being swept aside by the spreading of technology. It also accounts for the nervousness we feel at the prospect of being pushed to the margins of the pattern of technology when our skills become obsolete or our job is eliminated. Outside of the device paradigm there is less and less that commands wide respect. And our implication in technology explains the invidiousness that has invaded our culture. If the blessings of technology fail to provide genuine happiness, one may still hope to be relatively happy, securing a disproportionate claim on the fruits of technology and contemplating with some sort of satisfaction the unhappiness of the less fortunate.

As long as our implication in technology is not explicated, considered, and transformed, the heart of contemporary culture will be ailing—not mortally, for better or worse, but chronically and sullenly.

Is there an alternative to the pattern of technology? As Thomas Kuhn has taught us, people will not let go of a ruling paradigm unless or until a viable counterparadigm is on the horizon.[18] To see that there are in fact counterforces to the device paradigm abroad in contemporary culture, let us return to the distinction between reading and watching television. People continue to read good books. Norman Maclean's *A River Runs Through It and Other Stories* first became a best-seller through one reader's recommendation of it to another. Many readers have professed, moreover, that the book or its lead story has made a more profound and enduring impression on them than the film of the same name. How can it be that something so austere as a text can be more powerful than a film when a film provides information that is richer by orders of magnitude than the corresponding text?

If we assume that a large effect requires a large if distributed cause, where does the powerful effect of a printed story come from? The answer is that literacy on the part of the reader generates the wealth of information a viewer receives without charge. Literacy is a many-storied skill, rising from word recognition via parsing to comprehension. To read comprehendingly is to follow the author's instruction in the construction of an imaginary world. The author gives us the blueprint, but we must supply the materials and situate the structure. The materials are our experiences as well as our aspirations, in Maclean's case our knowledge of streams and forests, of family, of helplessness and consolation. The location of the structure is somewhere in the life of our imagination, that realm of pregnant possibility that surrounds and informs our actual life. Thus to read is to gather our past and illuminate our present. It is a focal activity that collects our world as a convex lens does and radiates back into our world as does a concave mirror.

A great film undoubtedly can do the same thing, and a cheap novel no doubt will fail to do it. The brain of every mainstream philosopher has been programmed to react to whatever general claim by racing through its instances in search of devastating counterexamples. While this is a fine exercise for graduate students, it prevents the mature philosopher from comprehending the subtle and crucial tendencies of contemporary culture. One such trend is that commodities by their very structure tend to lull and dull our senses and talents. Another trend is that certain things and practices provoke and engage our physical and moral gifts. The things I have in mind are good books, musical instruments, athletic equipment, works of art, and treasures of nature. The practices I am thinking of are those of dining, running, fishing, gardening, playing instruments, and reciting poetry. On closer inspection some such thing and a practice are always correlated. These are focal things and practices in the small and communal celebrations in the large.

124

Once the notion of focal concerns and communal celebrations has been clarified, it becomes evident that the pattern of the technological device is the ruling but certainly not the sole cultural force today. There is a literature of focal things and practices and of communal celebrations that testifies to the extent and vigor of an alternative reality.[19] It will be clear also that in most cases consumption of commodities and engagement in focal practices are found in one and the same life. But they cannot substitute for one another, and if one expands, the other must shrink.

The history of modern culture is obviously one of the expansion of the device paradigm and the fracturing and scattering of focal practices and communal celebrations. Focal things today are found in a diaspora. They are for the most part officially ignored and diffidently defended. On occasion concern for them surfaces unexpectedly. In the *New York Times* of 12 December 1995 the architect Hugh Hardy is fulsomely praised, as well he might be, for his restoration of architectural treasures. All this is done in the genteel discourse of high-culture consumption when suddenly the language gains in gravity, and we read:

> Mr. Hardy said he believes that it is the vitality of its public spaces that keeps a city healthy enough to counter the mounting popularity of simulated experience—theme parks as well as enclosed shopping malls— over the real thing.

> "People used to understand that gathering in public was good; that's what democracy meant," said Mr. Hardy.[20]

The distinction between "simulated experience" and "the real thing" is one that seems easily understood and is often made. But unlike the distinctions of liberalism vs. conservatism, pro-choice vs. pro-life, environmentalism vs. industrialism, the distribution vs. the aggregation of wealth, this one has no standing in the public forum, and this is what one should expect given the imbalance between the prominence of commodities and the dispersion of focal things.

It would be churlish to belittle the centering and animating power that can flow from the culture of the word and the culture of the table. But the orienting force of regularly reading poetry and sitting down to dinner trails off all too quickly in the thickets of moral confusions and cultural ambiguities. For Christians, however, it is but a short step from the culture of the word to the Word of God and from the culture of the table to the Breaking of the Bread. The history of salvation that is set out in Scripture and centered in the Eucharist certainly provides for the scope and coherence that the diaspora of focal things and communal celebrations is lacking.

In a practical sense religion enables some Americans to do the right thing. But ever since Anselm prevailed over Peter Damian, the church has agreed that doing the right thing benefits from thinking through the natural and cultural conditions that provide the setting for faithful action. Considering those conditions today, one cannot help but notice how thin the compass of religion has become. Why is its formative power so slight in our culture?

A culture informed by the device paradigm is deeply inhospitable to grace and sacrament. The productive side of technology is an enterprise of conquering and controlling reality. The notions of human incompleteness and deficiency that signify a primal condition for the advent of grace are mere grist for technological mills. On the side of consumption, the paradigmatic object is the instantaneously and easily available commodity. The notion that some *opus*, properly *operatum*, some thing, properly done, could exert power over us rather than our controlling it is foreign to the culture of consumption.

The ontological status of a sacrament is a problem I am not in a position to shed much light on. I merely want to note how problematic it has become under the rule of technology. The device paradigm, I am afraid, has not just taken cultural territory from the sacraments and left them untouched in their narrower sphere. By transforming the very notion of what is real it has likely clouded the very reality of the sacraments. In the recent *Catechism of the Catholic Church*, little is left of the tangible heft and gravity of the *opus*, and the emphasis has shifted to the *operatio* that can be conveniently abstracted from its material setting.[21] This theological attenuation is unhappily mirrored in contemporary Catholic liturgy where prayerful attitudes are safely elevated above the standards of excellence by which we used to measure tangible and audible things such as architecture and music.[22]

How then do we go about the task of thinking through the relation of Scripture and the sacraments to the culture of technology? To begin with the sacraments, the goal cannot be somehow to improve or adjust them so that they better meet the requirements of contemporary culture. The task is rather to make room for them and to do so in the circumspect way that Heidegger more than half a century ago sketched this way:

Only from the truth of Being can the essence of the holy be thought.
Only from the essence of the holy is the essence of divinity to be

thought. Only in light of the essence of divinity can it be thought or said what the word "God" is to signify.[23]

The truth of Being, we might say, is that reality today is ruled by the device paradigm and therefore inhospitable to the holy. In a society where the sense for the sacred has largely atrophied, sacraments are unlikely to have a focal place. Thus as Christians we must be concerned to strengthen reverence and piety wherever we find it: the natural piety of environmentalists, the aesthetic reverence of the arts community, the sense of wonder in the sciences. Proceeding from the holy to the divine, we should support the intimations of divinity that are diffidently celebrated in our society. I mean those occasions where people gather to be entertained and end up being inspired by the grace of an athletic event or an artistic performance that supervenes on everyone as an unexpected and undeserved gift.

As for Scripture, Christians cannot be unconcerned about the decay of the culture of the word and the thoughtless dismissal it is suffering at the hands of cyberspace enthusiasts. If generally to read is to gather one's past and to illuminate the present, this is eminently true of reading the Bible. Though sacred Scriptures do not have the same function in all denominations and religions, for Christians, at any rate, holy texts are a bond that unites the generations of believers into the people of God. But that bond is likely to fray if not break in a culture that neglects or derides thoughtful reading and listening.

It is most important to recognize that making contemporary culture more hospitable to sacrament and Scripture is not primarily a labor of sensitizing, of making people more receptive in a passive sense. What needs to be recovered is the skill of celebration. The union of discipline and grace that marks celebration has been divided by the device paradigm. Discipline has been assimilated to the machinery side and has turned into the strain and exertion of labor. Grace has been absorbed by the commodity side and has degenerated into the gratification of consumption. Celebration has, as a consequence, lost much of its discipline and is too often thought to be a matter of gratification rather than grace. This development has in some quarters enfeebled liturgy. There is no grace without discipline. Self-indulgence sometimes pervades the musical and tangible setting of the Eucharist. Thus as we move from the culture of technology via the secular culture of the sacred and the divine to the precincts of the sacraments, one thing we need to acquire and bring along is a sense of discipline and excellence when it comes to celebration.

Unless we join Heidegger in his coy reserve about the presence of God, we must move not only inward from the culture at large toward the center of religion but also outward from the focal point of the Breaking of the Bread to its cultural context. This is no doubt the more difficult move. At the level of partners and parents it comes to affirming on Monday what has been professed on Sunday. If the sacrament of the Eucharist is not reenacted in the sacramental (the sacrament's little sibling) of the dinner table, the Breaking of the Bread has a precarious place in contemporary culture. It is "intrinsically evil," Catholics are told, to use contraception.[24] I have never heard that said of the failure regularly to sit down to dinner, a morally much more consequential calamity. Men, as a rule, are the sinners here. Their contributions to the preparation and scheduling of dinner tend to be deplorable or worse.[25]

The culture of the word and its reflection of the Word of God require still more attention. A family needs to eat every evening and so is daily reminded of the dinner table if not regularly gathered around it. But there is no similarly persistent reminder of reading.

To move, as a matter of public policy, from the center of faith to the culture at large, we need to lower the wall between church and state. Such a suggestion, to be sure, runs squarely into the liberal fear of intolerance and the Protestant disdain of secular culture. These, again, are complex issues that I will only engage to conclude my remarks. We should certainly try to oblige liberal apprehensions by renouncing the zealous and imperial postures that religious people sometimes strike when they address the culture at large. Like the Italian bishops, we should allow the liturgy to be seen "as a cultural event."[26] And mindful of the religious diversity in the United States, we should invite our Jewish and Muslim friends and all religious people of goodwill to do likewise.

Leaving the wall between church and state intact is to reduce the force of religion in everyday life to an often ineffective overlay of moral exhortation. Meanwhile the material culture on the secular side of the barrier is left to the commandments and blessings of the device paradigm. This predicament is made worse by the in-your-face Christianity of some critics of contemporary culture for whom preaching the gospel comes mainly to scolding the middle class.

What the middle class is calling for is a promise of daily freedom and well-being that breaks with the device paradigm and holds out a sacramental life invigorated by a continuity of sacraments and sacramentals, of worship, of focal things and practices, and of communal celebrations. Let us be bearers of good news.

Notes ■

Introduction

1. John L. Allen Jr., "European Synod," *National Catholic Reporter*, 24 September 1999, pp. 3–4; Frank J. Tipler, *The Physics of Immortality* (New York: Anchor Books, 1995), pp. 343–48.

2. Robert D. Putnam, *Bowling Alone* (New York: Simon and Schuster, 2000), pp. 69–78.

3. Edward J. Larson and Larry Witham, "Scientists and Religion in America," *Scientific American*, September 1999, pp. 88–93; Putnam, *Bowling*, pp. 73–74.

4. Philip Jenkins, "A New Christendom," *Chronicle of Higher Education*, 29 March 2002, pp. B7–B10.

Chapter 1: The Invisibility of Contemporary Culture

1. See the index of *Scientific American*, December 2001, pp. 101–3.

2. See my "Does Philosophy Matter?" *Technology in Society*, 17 (1995), pp. 295–309.

3. *Scientific American*, December 2001, pp. 101–3.

4. For a more comprehensive effort, see my *Technology and the Character of Contemporary Life* (Chicago: University of Chicago Press, 1984).

5. Robert Farrar Capon disagrees. About margarine and butter, the siblings of Cool Whip and whipped cream, he says: "Any man who cannot tell the difference between butter and margarine has callouses on the inside of his mouth. Margarine *is* grease. It never achieves real liquidity upon the tongue; accordingly it leaves a coating where butter leaves none, and betrays itself every time." *Supper of the Lamb* (Garden City, N.Y.: Doubleday, 1969), p. 150.

6. All information about Cool Whip comes from its container.

7. Capon, *Supper*, pp. 42–43.

8. Dorothy Hartley, *Lost Country Life* (New York: Pantheon, 1979), p. 5.

9. *New York Times Magazine*, 17 February 1985, p. 52.

10. Ibid., p. 53.

11. Ibid., p. 41.

12. *New York Times Magazine*, 31 March 2002, inside front cover and p. 3, p. 17, and inside back cover.

13. Ibid., inside front cover.

14. *New York Times Magazine*, 17 February 1985, p. 65. All of the following quotations are from this page.

15. On this kind of leisureliness, see Lawrence Haworth, *Decadence and Objectivity* (Toronto: University of Toronto Press, 1977), pp. 137–51.

16. Michael Walzer, *Spheres of Justice* (New York: Basic Books, 1983); Charles Taylor, *Sources of the Self* (Cambridge: Harvard University Press, 1989).

Chapter 2: The Moral Significance of Material Culture

1. Carl Mitcham, "Three Ways of Being-With Technology," in *From Artifact to Habitat*, ed. Gayle L. Ormiston (Bethlehem, Pa.: Lehigh University Press, 1990), pp. 31–59.

2. Hans Jonas, "The Practical Uses of Theory," in *The Phenomenon of Life* (New York: Dell Publishing, 1966), pp. 188–210.

3. Richard Rorty, *Philosophy and the Mirror of Nature* (Princeton: Princeton University Press, 1979).

4. Martin Heidegger, *Sein und Zeit*, 9th ed. (Tübingen: Niemeyer, 1960 [1927]); Michael Oakeshott, *Rationalism in Politics* (New York: Basic Books, 1962).

5. Jaegwon Kim, "The Myth of Nonreductive Materialism," *Proceedings and Addresses of the American Philosophical Association* 63 (1989), pp. 31–47.

6. Suzi Gablik, *The Reenchantment of Art* (New York: Thames and Hudson, 1991).

7. Herbert Marcuse, *One-Dimensional Man* (Boston: Beacon, 1964), pp. 2, 16, 18, 235; John Rawls, *A Theory of Justice* (Cambridge: Harvard University Press, 1971), pp. 424–33.

8. Mary Douglas and Baron Isherwood, *The World of Goods* (New York: Basic Books, 1979).

9. See in particular p. 89 of Douglas and Isherwood, *The World of Goods*.

10. E.g., August Heckscher, *The Public Happiness* (New York: Atheneum, 1962); Walter Kerr, *The Decline of Pleasure* (New York: Simon and Schuster, 1962); Staffan B. Linder, *The Harried Leisure Class* (New York: Columbia University Press, 1970); Daniel J. Boorstin, *Democracy and Its Discontents* (New York: Vintage Books, 1975); Tibor Scitovsky, *The Joyless Economy* (Oxford: Oxford University Press, 1976); Robert L. Heilbroner, *An Inquiry into the Human Prospect*, 2d ed. (New York: Norton, 1980); Neil Postman, *Technopoly* (New York: Knopf, 1992); Robert Lane, *The Loss of Happiness in Market Economics* (New Haven: Yale University Press, 2001).

11. Mihaly Csikszentmihalyi and Eugene Rochberg-Halton, *The Meaning of Things* (New York: Cambridge University Press, 1981), pp. 1 and 46–47.

12. Ibid, p. 12.

13. Ibid., p. 43.

14. Ibid., pp. 32, 65, 77, 87, 178.

15. Ibid., pp. 55–89.

16. Ibid., p. 165.

17. Ibid., p. 58.

18. Ibid., p. 73.

19. Martha S. Hill, "Patterns of Time Use," in *Time, Goods, and Well-Being*, ed. F. Thomas Juster and Frank P. Stafford (Ann Arbor: Survey Research Center, Institute for Social Research, University of Michigan, 1985), p. 173. These data from the mid-seventies lump music, drama, and dance together, showing 0.07 mean hours per week for adults in this category and 0.39 for tapes and records. The spread of compact discs, personal stereos, and MTV has complicated the issue since then and may have reduced the performance of music. See John Robinson and Geoffrey Godbey, *Time for Life* (University Park: Pennsylvania State University Press, 1997), pp. 180–81. See also pp. 179 and 323.

20. Thomas S. Smith, "Late Nineteenth-Century Communications: Techniques and Machines," in *Technology in Western Civilization*, ed. Melvin Kranzberg and Carroll W. Pursell, Jr. (New York: Oxford University Press, 1967), vol 1, pp. 646–48.

21. Csikszentmihalyi and Rochberg-Halton, *The Meaning of Things*, pp. 71–72; see also pp. 243–44.

22. Ibid., p. 73.

23. Ibid., p. 115.

24. Ibid., p. 115.

25. Ibid., pp. 189–95.

26. Ibid., p. 193.

27. Ibid., pp. 195 and 243–44.

Chapter 3: Communities of Celebration

1. See Amy Gutmann, "Communitarian Critics of Liberalism," *Philosophy and Public Affairs*, 14 (1985), pp. 308–322; Don Herzog, "Some Questions for Republicans," *Political Theory*, 14 (1986), pp. 473–93; H. N. Hirsch, "The Threnody of Liberalism: Constitutional Liberty and the Renewal of Community," *Political Theory*, 14 (1986), pp. 423–49; Christopher Lasch, "The Communitarian Critique of Liberalism," *Soundings*, 69 (1986), pp. 60–76; Michael Sandel, "The State and the Soul," *New Republic*, 10 June 1985, pp. 37–41; Philip Selznick, "The Idea of a Communitarian Morality," *California Law Review*, 75 (1987), pp. 445–63. Samuel Walker, *The Rights Revolution* (New York: Oxford University Press, 1998), pp. 144–79. Here is a list of further communitarians, identified by one or more of the foregoing authors (in parentheses): Jerrold Auerbach (Hirsch), Benjamin Barber (Gutmann, Selznick), Richard John Neuhaus (Sandel), Quentin Skinner (Herzog), Thomas Spragen (Lasch), Jeffrey Stout (Lasch), William M. Sullivan (Selznick), Charles Taylor (Gutmann, Selznick), Lawrence Tribe (Hirsch), Roberto Mangabeira Unger (Gutmann, Selznick), Robert Paul Wolff (Selznick). I would add Christopher Lasch and George F. Will.

2. Henry Sumner Maine, *Ancient Law* (London: John Murray, 1912 [1861]), pp. 123–74; Ferdinand Tönnies, *Gemeinschaft und Gesellschaft* (Darmstadt, Germany: Wissenschaftliche Buchgesellschaft, 1979 [1887]), pp. 7–33.

3. Peter Laslett, *The World We Have Lost*, 3rd ed. (New York: Scribner, 1984).

4. For the description and discussion of such a festal occasion, see Erwin Panofsky, *Abbot Suger on the Abbey Church of St. Denis*, 2d ed., ed. Gerda Panofsky-Soergel (Princeton: Princeton University Press, 1979); and Otto von Simson, *The Gothic Cathedral*, 2d ed. (Princeton: Princeton University Press, 1962), pp. 129–41.

5. See Richard Sennett, *The Fall of Public Man* (New York: Knopf, 1977), pp. 45–122.

6. Ibid., pp. 123–255.

7. See my *Technology and the Character of Contemporary Life* (Chicago: University of Chicago Press, 1984), pp. 33–113.

8. Sennett, pp. 141–149.

9. Ibid., pp. 197–218.

10. Ada Louise Huxtable scored this hypertrophy in "Creeping Gigantism in Manhattan," *New York Times*, 22 March 1987, section 2, pp. 1 and 36. In the *New York Times Magazine* of that same day, on p. 52, James F. Clarity, in "Softball Immortality," told of communities of celebration that continue to lead a marginal life in the shadow of these gigantic structures.

11. See Thomas Huff, "Thinking Clearly About Privacy," *Washington Law Review* 51 (1980), pp. 785–86; and Judith W. Decew, "Defending the 'Private' in Constitutional Privacy," *Journal of Value Inquiry*, 21 (1987), pp. 171–84.

12. Huff, pp. 779, 786, and passim.

13. Ibid., pp. 777–94.

14. Ibid., p. 780.

15. Parker Palmer has noted this curious inconsistency in "The Nature and Nurture of Public Life," *Kettering Review*, 47 (fall 1986).

16. As Lasch emphasizes, pp. 73–74.

17. See "Going for the Green," *Time*, 18 June 1984, pp. 60–61; "In Olympics, Business Also Goes for the Gold," *U.S. News and World Report*, 23 June 1984, pp. 73–74; Jacob Weisberg, "Gross National Production," *New Republic*, 23 June 1986, pp. 19–23.

18. John Kenneth Galbraith, *The New Industrial State* (Boston: Houghton, 1967).

19. See my "Reply to Professor Carpenter and to Professor Stanley," in *Philosophy and Technology*, 4 (1988), pp. 29–43.

20. Regarding commercialization, see the references in note 17 and "The Lady's Party," *Time*, 14 July 1986, p. 10.

21. Fred Hirsch, *Social Limits to Growth* (Cambridge: Harvard University Press, 1976), pp. 71–114.

22. See "Going for the Goose Bumps," *Newsweek*, 26 March 1984, p. 78; "Wolper: Impresario of the Big Event," *Newsweek*, 7 July 1986, p. 19; and Weisberg, pp. 19–20.

23. For a study of the contrast between a genuine communal celebration and one that is technologically procured, see Herman W. Konrad, "Barren Bulls and Charging Cows: Cowboy Celebrations in Copal and Calgary," in *The Celebration of Society*, ed. Frank E. Manning (Bowling Green: Bowling Green University Popular Press, 1983), pp. 145–164.

24. See Robert D. McFadden, "Miss Liberty Reopens Amid Gaiety in the Harbor," *New York Times*, 6 July 1986, pp. 1 and 16; Samuel G. Freedman, "A Cheerful Celebration of the Good-Hearted American Idyll," ibid., p. 17.

25. See my *Technology*, pp. 107–113; and my "Reply," in notes 7 and 19 above.

26. On the many (94 actually) meanings of community, see George A. Hillery, "Definitions of Community: Areas of Agreement," *Rural Sociology*, 20 (1955), pp. 111–23.

27. Robert N. Bellah et al., *Habits of the Heart* (Berkeley: University of California Press, 1984), pp. 333, 335, and passim.

28. See Don Handelman, "Play and Ritual: Complementary Frames of Meta-Communication," in *It's a Funny Thing, Humour*, ed., Antony J. Chapman and Hugh C. Foot (Oxford: Pergamon, 1977), pp. 185–192.

29. Clifford Geertz, "Deep Play: Notes on the Balinese Cockfight," *Daedalus*, 101 (1972), pp. 1–37.

30. Ibid., p. 5.

31. Lawrence Haworth, *The Good City* (Bloomington: Indiana University Press, 1963), p. 145.

32. See Palmer, p. 51; and Marshall Berman, "Take It to the Streets: Conflict and Community in Public Space," *Dissent*, fall 1986, pp. 484–485.

33. Michael Walzer, "Pleasures and Costs of Urbanity," *Dissent*, fall 1986, pp. 470–71.

34. Michael Rustin, "The Fall and Rise of Public Space: A Postcapitalist Prospect," *Dissent*, fall 1986, p. 493.

35. Berman, p. 483.

36. Ibid., pp. 478, 480, 483–84.

37. See the references in note 4.

38. See William A. Galston, "Public Morality and Religion in the Liberal State," *Political Science*, 19 (1986), pp. 807–24.

39. For an account of the misgivings that divide artists and the Catholic Church, see Tim McCarthy, "'The Church and the Artist': Salvaging a Stormy Love Affair from the Rocks," *National Catholic Reporter*, 18 September 1987, pp. 9–15.

40. See "The Awakening of a Cathedral," *Newsweek*, 16 June 1986, pp. 59–60; and Ari L. Goldman, "More Than a Cathedral: St. John the Divine," *New York Times Magazine*, part 2, 15 November 1987, pp. 22–25, 74–76.

41. For an explication of leisureliness, see Lawrence Haworth, *Decadence and Objectivity* (Toronto: University of Toronto Press, 1977), pp. 144–46.

42. Lasch, p. 67; see also Robert Bellah, "A Response: The Idea of Practices in Habits," *Soundings*, 69 (spring/summer 1986), p. 183.

43. Michael J. Sandel, "Morality and the Liberal State," *New Republic*, 7 May 1984, p. 17; and Robert Putnam, *Bowling Alone* (New York: Simon and Schuster, 2000), pp. 351–58.

44. See Galston, "Public Morality," pp. 810–12, 819, 822; and Walter B. Mead, "How Strict Was 'Separation' of Church and State?" *Cross Currents*, 23 (1986), pp. 244–47.

45. Lasch, p. 66.

46. See Jean Bethke Elshtain, *Public Man, Private Woman* (Princeton: Princeton University Press, 1981), pp. 342–48; H. N. Hirsch, "Threnody"; Ronald Dworkin, "To Each His Own," *New York Review of Books*, 14 April 1983, pp. 4–6; Walker, *The Rights Revolution*.

47. Michael Walzer, *Spheres of Justice* (New York: Basic Books, 1983), pp. 3–63.

48. Sennett, p. 288.

49. Ibid., pp. 289–93.

50. Bellah et al., pp. 71–75.

51. Cf. Berman's concern in "Take It," pp. 480–83.

52. Sennett, pp. 257–340.

53. Palmer, pp. 52–53; Haworth, *The Good City*, pp. 105, 158; Walzer, *Spheres*, p. 470.

54. See Hannah Arendt, *The Human Condition* (Chicago: University of Chicago Press, 1958), pp. 38–39.

55. Here is a contact with liberal theory. Cf. John Rawls's notion of social union in *A Theory of Justice* (Cambridge: Harvard University Press, 1971), pp. 520–29.

56. This point is approximately made by Walzer, "The Pleasures and Costs," p. 474; and by Rustin, p. 493.

57. Walzer, *Spheres*, pp. 281–82; Putnam, *Bowling*, pp. 148–66.

58. Cf. Galston's defense of a moment of silence in public schools in "Public Morality," p. 822.

59. Cf. Haworth, *The Good City*, pp. 53–62, 102–28.

60. René Descartes, *Discourse on Method*, trans. Laurence J. Lafleur (Indianapolis: Bobbs, 1950), pp. 7–11. "Urban Planning: What Went Wrong?" *U.S. News and World Report*, 30 March 1987, pp. 76–77.

61. Quoted by William Glaberson, "A Sense of Limits Grips Consumers," *New York Times*, 15 March 1987, section 3, p. 14.

62. Hope and help can be found in Kent C. Bloomer and Charles W. Moore, *Body, Memory and Architecture* (New Haven: Yale University Press, 1977).

63. Elshtain, pp. 204–28 and 322–37.

64. See my *Technology*, pp. 196–210.

65. Ibid., pp. 226–27.

66. See Carol Gilligan, *In a Different Voice* (Cambridge: Harvard University Press, 1982).

Chapter 4: Contingency and Grace

1. Quoted in Edward J. Larson and Larry Witham, "Scientists and Religion in America," *Scientific American*, September 1999, p. 90.

2. Steven Weinberg, "A Designer Universe?" *New York Review of Books*, 21 October 1999, p. 48.

3. Rosalind Hursthouse, *On Virtue Ethics* (Oxford: Oxford University Press, 1999), p. 243. Her profession of theism is on p. 265.

4. See to the contrary, John Leslie, *Universes* (London: Routledge, 1989); and John Polkinghorne, *The Faith of a Physicist* (Minneapolis: Fortress, 1996).

5. Isaac Newton, letter to Richard Bentley, 10 December 1692, in *Theories of the Universe*, ed. Milton K. Munitz, (New York: Free Press, 1957), p. 212.

6. Penny Fannia, "From Stardust Shroud, an Astral Child," available at <www.theage.com.au/cgi-bin/print_article.pl?path=/news/2001/02/22/ FFXCVT0WFJC.html> on 2 July 2001.

7. Henry Adams, *The Education of Henry Adams* (New York: Modern Library, 1996 [1918]), p. 225.

8. Reported by Augustus De Morgan in *A Budget of Paradoxes*, 2d ed., ed. David Eugene Smith (Freeport, N.Y.: Books for Libraries, 1969 [1915], vol. 2, pp. 1–2.

9. Leslie, *Universes*, p. 32.

10. Steven Weinberg, "Can Science Explain Everything? Anything?" *New York Review of Books*, 31 May 2001, p. 50.

11. Steven Weinberg in an interview available at <www.meta-library.net/transcript/wein-body.html> on 15 May 2001.

12. Richard Dawkins, *The Blind Watchmaker* (New York: Norton, 1996), p. 144.

13. Daniel C. Dennett, *Darwin's Dangerous Idea* (New York: Simon and Schuster, 1995), p. 71.

14. Stephen H. Kellert, *In the Wake of Chaos* (Chicago: University of Chicago Press, 1993), p. 47.

15. Polkinghorne, *Faith*, pp. 25–26, 68, 78, 150.

16. Kellert, *In the Wake*, p. 116.

17. Stephen Jay Gould, *Rocks of Ages: Science and Religion in the Fullness of Life* (New York: Ballantine, 1999), p. 5.

18. Dennett, *Darwin's Dangerous Idea*, p. 154.

19. Dawkins, *Blind Watchmaker*, p. 5.

20. Ibid., xiii.

21. Steven Weinberg, *Dreams of a Final Theory* (New York: Pantheon, 1992), p. 165; see also pp. 6, 17, 90, 98, 104, 107, 132–65, 167.

22. Ibid., pp. 149–150.

23. Quoted by James Glanz in "Physicist Ponders God, Truth and 'A Final Theory,'" *New York Times*, 25 January 2000, section F, p. 1.

24. Dennett, *Darwin's Dangerous Idea*, p. 23.

25. Ibid., p. 520.

26. Steven Weinberg, *The First Three Minutes*, 2d ed. (New York: Basic Books, 1993), p. 154.

27. Daniel C. Dennett, "Real Patterns," *Journal of Philosophy*, 88 (1991), pp. 27–51.

28. Weinberg, *Dreams*, p. 250.

29. Glanz, "Physicist," p. 1; Weinberg, "Can Science Explain?" p. 50.

30. Weinberg, *First Three Minutes*, p. 155.

31. John Rawls, *A Theory of Justice*, 2d ed. (Cambridge: Harvard University Press, 1999), p. 514.

32. Karl Rahner, *Nature and Grace* (New York: Sheed and Ward, 1964), 133. See also his *Alltagliche Dinge* (Einsiedeln: Benziger, 1964).

33. Polkinghorne, *Faith*, p. 78.

34. Kellert, *In the Wake*, pp. 119–58.

35. Martha Nussbaum, "Human Functioning and Social Justice," *Political Theory*, 20 (1992), p. 203.

36. Josiah Royce, *Race Questions, Provincialism and Other American Problems* (New York: Macmillan, 1908), p. 173.

37. Robert D. Putnam, *Bowling Alone* (New York: Simon and Schuster, 2000).

38. E. M. Forster, "The Machine Stops," in *The Collected Tales of E. M. Forster* (New York: Knopf, 1947), pp. 144–97.

39. Roger Scruton, "The End of Courage: The Strange Death of an Old Virtue," available at <www.philosophynews.com/philosopheye/ARCHIVED/pheye990604.htm> on 14 August 2000.

Chapter 5: Power and Care

1. I owe some of my uneasiness about this approach along with my understanding of fundamental theology to Bernhard Welte, *Auf der Spur des Ewigen* (Freiburg im Breisgau, Germany: Herder, 1965).

2. See Martin Heidegger, *The Question Concerning Technology*, trans. William Lovitt (New York: Harper and Row, 1977); *Identity and Difference*, trans. Joan Stambaugh (New York: Harper and Row, 1969); and *The Piety of Thinking*, trans. James G. Hart and John C. Maraldo (Bloomington: Indiana University Press, 1976).

3. See Karl Rahner, *Hörer des Wortes*, rev. ed., ed. Johannes Baptist Metz (Freiburg im Breisgau, Germany: Herder, 1971). Here too I have been a beneficiary of the attempt to break new ground without being able to accept the particulars of the enterprise.

4. Terry J. Tekippe, "Bernard Lonergan: A Context for Technology," in *Theology and Technology*, ed. Carl Mitcham and Jim Grote (Lanham, Md.: University Press of America, 1984), pp. 71–90.

5. George W. Shields, "Process Theology and Technology," *Theology and Technology*, pp. 279–90.

6. Bill Joy, "Why the Future Doesn't Need Us," available at <www.wired.com/wired/archive/8.04/joy_pr.html> on 3 March 2002; Francis Fukuyama, "Biotechnology and the Threat of a Posthuman Future," *Chronicle of Higher Education*, 22 March 2002, pp. B7–B10.

7. Cf. Peter Laslett, *The World We Have Lost*, 3rd ed. (New York: Scribner, 1984), pp. 122–52.

8. The plausibility of this expectation is argued by Alvin M. Weinberg in "Can Technology Replace Social Engineering?" in *Technology and the Future*, ed. Albert H. Teich (New York: St. Martin's Press, 1993), pp. 30–39.

9. Cf. Bernhard Welte, *Über das Wesen und den rechten Gebrauch der Macht* (Freiburg im Breisgau, Germany: Rombach, 1960), particularly pp. 41–49.

Chapter 6: Liberty, Festivity, and Poverty

1. Harvey Cox, *The Secular City* (New York: Macmillan, 1966); *The Feast of Fools* (Cambridge: Harvard University Press, 1969); and *Religion in the Secular City* (New York: Simon and Schuster, 1984).

2. Robert M. Pirsig, *Zen and the Art of Motorcycle Maintenance* (New York: Morrow, 1974).

3. See Paul Lehmann's appreciation of the promise of redemption in "Chalcedon in Technopolis," in *The Secular City Debate*, ed. Daniel Callahan (New York: Macmillan, 1966) pp. 64–68.

4. Cox, *The Secular City*, p. 38.

5. The affinity to the Enlightenment, entirely implicit in the *Secular City*, has been noted by Michael Novak in *The Secular City Debate*, p. 109, and has been acknowledged by Cox ibid., pp. 118–19 and 212.

6. *The Secular City*, p. 51.

7. Ibid., pp. 54–59.

8. *The Feast of Fools*, pp. 3–18.

9. Ibid., p. 15.

10. Ibid., pp. 48–55.

11. *Religion in the Secular City*, pp. 144–46.

12. See John A. Coleman, "The Revival of God," *New York Times Book Review*, 4 March 1984, p. 37; and J. M. Cameron, "Meeting the Lord in the Air," *New York Review of Books*, 11 October 1984, p. 40.

13. *Religion in the Secular City*, p. 184.

14. Ibid., pp. 185–88.

15. Ibid., p. 185.

16. Ibid., pp. 74–82.

17. Karl Rahner, "Theologische Deutung der Position des Christen in der modernen Welt," in *Sendung und Gnade* (Innsbruck, Austria: Tyrolia-Verlag, 1966), pp. 24–27.

Chapter 7: Courage and Fortitude

1. William Miller, *The Mystery of Courage* (Cambridge: Harvard University Press, 2000).

2. Rosalind Hursthouse, *On Virtue Ethics* (Oxford: Oxford University Press, 1999).

3. William J. Bennett, *The Book of Virtues* (New York: Simon and Schuster, 1993).

4. Aristotle, *Nicomachean Ethics*, book IX, ch. 8.

5. Ibid., Book III, ch. 6.

6. Kelly Rogers, "Aristotle's Conception of *To Kalon*," *Ancient Philosophy* 13 (1993), pp. 355–71.

7. Victor Davis Hanson, *The Western Way of War: Infantry Battle in Classical Greece*, 2d ed. (Berkeley: University of California Press, 2000).

8. *Nicomachean Ethics*, book III, ch. 8.

9. Thomas Aquinas, *Summa Theologica*, Second Part of the Second Part, question 123, article 5.

10. Ibid., article 6. Miller, *Mystery*, pp. 118–20.

11. Thomas, *Summa*, Second Part of the Second Part, question 124.

12. Miller, *Mystery*, pp. 264–65.

13. Karl Marx and Friedrich Engels, *The Communist Manifesto*, ed. Samuel H. Beer (New York: Appelton-Century-Crofts, 1955, [1848]), p. 13.

14. William James, "The Moral Equivalent of War" (1910), in *Essays on Faith and Morals*, ed. Ralph Barton Perry (Cleveland: World Publishing Company, 1962), p. 325.

15. Ibid.

16. Miller, *Mystery*, p. 283.

17. Robert D. Putnam, *Bowling Alone* (New York: Simon and Schuster, 2000).

18. Virginia Woolf, "A Sketch of the Past," *Moments of Being*, ed. Jeanne Schulkind (New York: Harcourt Brace Jovanovich, 1976), pp. 70–73.

Chapter 8: The Culture of the Word and the Culture of the Table

1. Barbara Ehrenreich, *Fear of Falling: The Inner Life of the Middle Class* (New York: Pantheon, 1989).

2. John Cassidy, "Who Killed the Middle Class?" *New Yorker*, 16 October 1995, pp. 113–24. Susan Sheehan, "Ain't No Middle Class," *New Yorker*, 11 December 1995, pp. 82–93.

3. Ehrenreich, *Fear*, pp. 29–38 and 223–31.

4. Charles McGrath, "The Triumph of the Prime-Time Novel," *New York Times Magazine*, 22 October 1995, p. 52.

5. McGrath, "Triumph," p. 55.

6. Ibid.

7. Ibid., p. 86.

8. Norman J. G. Pounds, *Hearth and Home: A History of Material Culture* (Bloomington: Indiana University Press, 1989).

9. Robert M. Crunden, *A Brief History of American Culture* (New York: Paragon, 1994).

10. Edward B. Tylor, *Primitive Culture*, 2 vols., 7th ed. (New York: Brentano, 1924 [1871]), vol. 1, p. 1.

11. Norman Maclean, "A River Runs Through It," *A River Runs Through It and Other Stories* (Chicago: University of Chicago Press, 1976), pp.1–104.

12. Maclean, "The Woods, Books, and Truant Officers," in *Norman Maclean*, ed. Ron McFarland and Hugh Nichols (Lewiston, Id.: Confluence Press, 1988), p. 84.

13. Maclean, "The Hidden Art of a Good Story," ibid., pp. 25–26 and "The Woods," pp. 82–83.

14. Maclean, "Montana Memory," ibid., p. 70. See also "The Hidden Art," p. 26 and "Teaching and Story Telling," ibid., pp. 90–91.

15. Maclean, "The Hidden Art," p. 26.

16. Marjorie L. DeVault, *Feeding the Family* (Chicago: University of Chicago Press, 1991).

17. A view, by the way, shared by the *Catechism of the Catholic Church* (Mahwah, N.J.: Paulist Press, 1994), p. 52 (sections 2293–94).

18. Thomas Kuhn, *The Structure of Scientific Revolutions* (Chicago: University of Chicago Press, 1962), pp. 110–58.

19. See my *Technology and the Character of Contemporary Life* (Chicago: University of Chicago Press, 1984), p. 201.

20. Julie V. Iovine, "Tenacity in the Service of Public Culture," *New York Times*, 12 December 1995, p. B4.

21. What little is left can be found in the sections titled "Signs and Symbols" (1145–52, pp. 296–98). The stress is entirely on the referent or tenor. Consider, to the contrary, the emphasis that is given to the sign or vehicle in *Universalis Catechismus Romanus* (Augsburg: Matthaeus Rieger, 1761), pp. 176–86.

22. On music see Thomas Day, *Why Catholics Can't Sing* (New York: Crossroad, 1993).

23. Martin Heidegger, "Letter on Humanism" (1947), in *Basic Writings*, ed. David Farrell Krell (New York: Harper, 1977), p. 230.

24. See *Catechism*, section 2370, p. 570.

25. See DeVault, *Feeding*.

26. "Italian Bishops Insist Mass Is a 'Cultural Event,'" *National Catholic Reporter*, 16 July 1993, p. 10.

Index ■

Adams, Henry 68
advertisements
    normative force of 21
    as praise of commodities 20–22
agnosticism among scientists 66
Allen, John L. Jr. 129n.1
Aquinas, Thomas 25–26, 112
Arendt, Hannah 133n.54
Aristotle 25, 110
ascesis, Christian 94
atheism
    and education 7
    common ground of Christianity with
        73–74
    and prosperity 7
    among scientists 66–67
    and technology 97
Atkins, Peter 66
Auerbach, Jerrold 131n.1
autonomy, cocoon of 115

Bach, Johann Sebastian 91
Barber, Benjamin 131n.1
Bell, David 113
Bellah, Robert 35, 47, 56
Bennett, William 110
Berman, Marshall 50
Bloomer, Kent C. 134n.62
Boorstin, Daniel J. 130n.10
Boston 96

Cameron, J. M. 137n.11 (ch. 6)
Capon, Robert Farrar 15–16, 129n.5
Cassidy, John 137n.2 (ch.8)
Catechism of the Catholic Church 126, 138n.17,
        138n.24

celebration
    dematerialization of 47–48
    as play 47
    real and focal 48
    as ritual 47
    as a social text 47
    See also communal celebration
chaos, deterministic 70–71
Christ
    imitation of 90
    as liberator 99
    and principle ethics 110
Christianity
    apparent end of 7–8, 97–98
    ascetic 94
    and its claim to exclusive salvation 97–98
    Cox on return of, to the city 102
    met with indifference 65
    in theory and practice 107–8
    and public sphere 128
Christian standards competing with techno-
        logical standards 82–84
church
    attendance 7
    imperialism of 128
church and state, separation of 52–53, 128
citizen vs. consumer 34
Clarity, James F. 132n.10
Coleman, John A. 137n.12 (ch.6)
commodification
    and mechanization 31
    of music 29–30, 33
commodity
    defined 17–18
    pervasiveness of 121
    rests on unintelligible machinery 122
    shallowness of 86–87

139

Index

communal celebration
   tennis as 52
   active and focused 50
   engaging 53
   limited by diffusion and passivity 49
   reality of 52
   reflective 53
   religious 53–54
communitarianism
   criticism of 36
   representatives of 35, 131n.1
communities of celebration
   instability of 58–59
   open membership in 57
   public support of 58–59
community
   defined 47
   vs. intimacy 57
   and tolerance 57–58
consumer vs. citizen 34
consumption as response to commodities 76
contingency
   defined 65
   and divinity 66–73
   in evolution 71–72
   negligible vs. commanding 72–73
   of scientifically ascertainable conditions
      68–70
   of scientific laws 67–68
Cool Whip 15–16, 22
cosmology 68–69
courage
   vs. fortitude 112
   moral 114
   psychological puzzles of 109
   and war 109–11
Cox, Harvey
   on celebration 100–1
   on conventional theology 97
   on liberty 96–99
   on the return of Christianity 102
   on secularization 96
   on urbanization 96
creation
   as donation rather than causation 73
   and regardless power 92
Crunden, Robert 119
Csikszentmihalyi, Mihaly 28–29, 32–33
culture
   descriptive sense of 119
   liturgy as 128

   normative sense of 119
contemporary
   American middle-class 117
   concealment of 11–13, 36–37, 117–19
   indifference of, to Christianity 65
   self-consciousness of 11
   of the sixties 101
   of the table
      and the breaking of the bread 125
      as reenactment of the Eucharist 128
   of technology, as ideal 95
   of the word
      decay of, and Scripture 127
      former vigor of 119–20
      vs. television 120–21
      and Word of God 125–26
      and world appropriation 31–32
curiosity, as a response to the references to
      reality 73

dailiness of life 84–85, 97, 114
Dawkins, Richard 69, 71–72, 73, 134n.12
Day, Thomas 138n.22
Decew, Judith W. 132n.11
decisions
   daily vs. fundamental 122–23
   made by consumer vs. made by citizen
      34
DeMott, Benjamin 23
Dennett, Daniel 69–70, 71, 72, 73
Descartes, René 134n.60
determinism as a view of technology 122
deterministic chaos 70–71
device paradigm
   defined 17–18, 31
   explanation of 121–22
   extensions of 18
DeVault, Marjorie L. 138n.16, 138n.25
discourse
   appropriate to nature and music 90–91
   cogent 90–93
   political 12
discrimination 56
Dworkin, Ronald 133n.46

Edison, Thomas A. 30
education and faith 7
Ehrenreich, Barbara 117–18, 137nn.1, 3
Einstein, Albert 11
Elshtain, Jean Bethke 61, 133n.46
Engels, Friedrich 112
Enlightenment 97

equality, not widely desired 45–46
ethics
    real 34
    practical 34
    principle 110–11
    theoretical 34
    virtue 110–11
evolution
    contingency in 71–72
    and careful explanation 68

feminism and celebration 62
First Amendment 52, 55
focal things
    dispersed in contemporary culture 125
    examples of 124
    proximity of in daily life 115
focal things and practices
    defined 22
    as counterforces to technology 27
Forster, E.M. 77
fortitude
    as defining virtue of postmodern era 116
    vs. courage 112
freedom See liberation, liberty
Freedman, Samuel G. 132n.24
Fukuyama, Francis 83
Gablik, Suzi 130n.6
Galbraith, John Kenneth 43
Galston, William 133n.44, 133n.38, 134n.58
Geertz, Clifford 47
Gilligan, Carol 134n.66
God
    the creator 69–70, 73
    grace as the presence of 65
    and the holy and divinity 126–27
Godbey, Geoffrey 131n.19
Goldman, Ari L. 133n.40
Gould, Stephen J. 71
grace
    actual 74
    and gratification 127
    habitual 74–75, 79–80
    marginalized by technology 126
    in moments of being 115
    personal 77, 79–80
    real 77, 79–80
    sacramental 74
    secular 73–74
    trouble as a twin of 78–79
    universal 74
Gutmann, Amy 131n.1

Handelman, Don 133n.28
Hanson, Victor Davis 137n.7 (ch.7)
Hardy, Hugh 125
Hartley, Dorothy 17
Hartshorne, Charles 83, 84
Haworth, Lawrence 48, 130n.15 (ch.1),
        133n.41
Heckscher, August 130n.10
Heidegger, Martin 27, 82, 126–27, 128
Heilbroner, Robert L. 130n.10
Herzog, Don 131n.1
Hill, Martha S. 131n.19
Hillery, George A. 132n.26
Hirsch, Fred 45
Hirsch, H. N. 131n.1, 133n.46
holy, realm of the 93–94. See also sacred
horse, as focal thing 23
Huff, Thomas 40, 41
human nature, reduction of 92
Hume, David 112
hunger 86
Hursthouse, Rosalind 67
Huxtable, Ada Louise 132n.10

Iacocca, Lee 42–43
implication in technology 122–23
incapacity for misery 105
Industrial Revolution 75–76
instrumentalism as a view of technology
        122–23
intimacy vs. community 57
intolerance
    communal 58
    technological 58

James, William 113
Jefferson, Thomas 52
Jenkins, Philip 129n.4
Jonas, Hans 130n.2
Joy, Bill 83

Kant, Immanuel 110
Kellert, Stephen H. 70–71, 75
Kennedy, John 96
Kerr, Walter 130n.10
Kim, Jaegwon 130n.5
Konrad, Herman W. 132n.23

labor
    expanding into public sphere in nine-
        teenth century 39
    in technology 87

Index

Lane, Robert 130n.10
Laplace, Pierre-Simon 68
Larson, Edward J. 129n.3
Lasch, Christopher 54, 55, 113, 131n.1
Laslett, Peter 131n.3, 136n.7 (ch. 5)
Lehmann, Paul 136n.3 (ch.6)
Leslie, John 68–69
liberalism
    and discrimination 56
    and religion 55–56, 128
liberation
    from the duress of reality 7
    in technology 98–99
liberty
    Cox on 96–99
    and human wholeness 99–100
    technology as the promise of 120–21
Linder, Staffan B. 130n.10
literacy 124
liturgy
    attenuation of 126, 127
    as culture 128
Liszt, Franz 39
Lonergan, Bernard 82–83, 84

machinery of the device paradigm
    defined 17–18
    explained 121–22
    unintelligible 122
MacIntyre, Alasdair 35
Maclean, Norman 119–20, 124
Maine, Henry Sumner 131n.2
Marcuse, Herbert 130n.7
Marx, Karl 112
material culture, elusiveness of 27–28
McCarthy, Tim 133n.39
McFadden, Robert D. 132n.24
McGrath, Charles 118
mechanization and commodification 31
middle class
    crisis of 117–18
    religious need of 128
Miller, Arthur 11
Miller, William 109, 111, 112, 113
misery
    resentment in the face of 85, 88–89
    unintelligible today 85
Mitcham, Carl 130n.1
mobility 98–99
Moore, Charles W. 134n.62
moral excellence, traditional 45–46

moral thresholds 115–16
music
    commanding presence of 29
    commodification of 29–31, 33
    as communal celebration 51–52
    engaging 32–33
    modern classical 50–51
    street corner 51–52
    and technology 56

Neuhaus, Richard John 131n.1
New Delhi 96
Newton, Isaac 11, 68
Nietzsche, Friedrich 113
Novak, Michael 136n.5 (ch. 6)
Nussbaum, Martha 75, 79

Oakeshott, Michael 27
Olympics 42–45
optimism, unwarranted, of the pessimists 83, 91

Paganini, Niccolò 39
Paley, William 71
Palmer, Parker 132n.15
Panofsky, Erwin 131n.4
Paul of Tarsus 90
pessimists, unwarranted optimism of 83, 91
philosophical theory, poverty of 26–27
philosophy
    contemporary
        commands no assent 12–13
        and culture 13
        implicated in contemporary culture 13
    modern
        aim of 26
        removed from real world 25–26
    of technology
        and contemporary culture 14
        exemplified 15
Pirsig, Robert 95–96
Plato 25
political discourse 12
politics
    communal 58–61
    and contemporary culture 12
    technological 60–61
Polkinghorne, John 71, 75
Pope, Alexander 68

Postman, Neil 130n.10
poverty
    advanced 104–7
    biblical 103
    brute 104–7
    Cox on 103
    reduced by technology 103–4
Pounds, J. G. 119
power
    careful 89–91
    regardless 88–89
practice
    Christian 107–8
    and theory 25–26
Prague 96
presence
    grace as, of God 65
    as a mode of reality 73
privacy
    rise of in the modern period 40–41
    See also public-private distinction
prosperity
    as specified by technology 38–39
    technology as the promise of 120–21
public-private distinction
    economic 41–46
    social 37–41
public sector 41–42
public space
    final 61
    instrumental 60–61
    transformation of in nineteenth century
        39
    in the twentieth century 39–40
Putnam, Robert 77, 115, 133n.43

Rahner, Karl 74, 107, 136n.3
Rawls, John 74, 130n.7, 134n.55
reading
    and the culture of the word 119–20
    power of 124
    vs. watching television 120–21
reality
    commanding 28–29, 77–78
    pliable or disposable 28–29
    as reference and as presence 73–74
    vs. simulation 125
    as a texture of laws and conditions 67–69
reference as a mode of reality 73–74
restlessness 78
reverence 127

ritual and celebration 47
Robinson, John 131n.19
Rochberg-Halton, Eugene 28–29, 32–33
Rogers, Kelly 137n.6 (ch. 7)
Rorty, Richard 130n.3
Rome 96
Royce, Josiah 76
Rustin, Michael 50

sacraments
    besieged by technology 126
    as *opera operata* (things done) 126
sacred
    the atrophied sense of 127
    See also holy
salvation
    Christianity's exclusive claim to 97–98
    incapacity for 86–87
    indifference to 85
    secular version of 87–88
Sandel, Michael 35, 54–55, 131n.1
sciences
    cogency of 11–12
    contemplative vs. technological 13–14
    implicated in contemporary culture
        13–14
    influence of, on philosophy 26
scientific laws, contingency of 67–68
scientists, atheism and agnosticism among
        66–67
Scitovsky, Tibor 130n.10
Scripture and the decay of the culture of the
        word 127
Scruton, Roger 78–79
secularization, Cox on 96
secular grace 73–74
secular version of salvation 87–88
Selznick, Philip 131n.1
Sennett, Richard 39, 45, 50, 56, 57
separation of church and state 128
September 11, 2001 109
Shakespeare, William 11
Sheehan, Susan 137n.2 (ch. 8)
Shields, George W. 83
Simson, Otto von 131n.4
simulation vs. reality 125
Skinner, Quentin 131n.1
Smith, Adam 112
Smith, Thomas S. 131n.20
Sousa, Ronald de 71
standard of living vs. faith 7

Index

Statue of Liberty, restoration of 42–45
St. John the Divine 54
subjectivity and arbitrariness 92–93

table *See* culture of the table
Taylor, Charles 130n.16 (ch. 1), 131n.1
technology
  as the adversary of courage 112–13
  beneficial 122
  besieges sacraments 126
  concealment of implication in 41
  constructive phase of 122
  culture of, as ideal 95
  as the culture of transparency and control
    66
  dailiness of 84–85, 86
  determinist view of 122
  vs. faith, 7–8
  elusiveness of 82
   as enriching 76
   expansion of 19
   implication in 122–23
   instrumentalist view of 122–23
   as isolating 77
   as liberating 75–76, 98–99
   marginalizes grace 126
   and metaphysics 82, 88
   moral character of 19
   norms of comfort and security in 85
   and poverty 103–4, 106
   as the promise of liberation 120–21
   as the promise of prosperity 120–21
   purposive chains in 84
   reform of 54
   restrained from the center of life 94
   self-correcting 83
   terminology for examination of 96
   theology of 81–82, 87
   vigorous and self-confident 35
  See also culture, contemporary conceal-
    ment of; device paradigm
Tekippe, Terry J. 83
television
  culture of 118–19
  in daily routine 114–15
tennis as communal celebration 52, 53
theodicy 79, 92

theology
  conventional, challenged by Cox 97
  practical 94
  of technology 81–82, 87
theory and practice 25–26
things, distinguished from devices 31–32
Thomas Aquinas 25–26, 112
thresholds, moral vs. physical 115–16
Tipler, Frank J. 129n.1
tolerance and community 58
Tönnies, Ferdinand 131n.2
Tribe, Lawrence 131
trouble
  accepted in principle and in practice 79
  grace as twin of 78
  rejected in principle, accepted in practice
    79
TWA 20–21
Tylor, E. B. 119

Ueberroth, Peter 42–43
Unger, Roberto Mangabeira 131n.1
Universalis Catechismus Romanus 138n.21
urbanization, Cox on 96

virtue
  as arduously acquired and faithfully
    maintained habit 116
  ethics of 110–11
  as moral skill 110–11

Walker, Samuel 131n.1, 133n.46
Walzer, Michael 35, 50, 52, 55, 130n.16 (ch.
  1)
war, the moral equivalent of 113
Weinberg, Alvin M. 136n.8 (ch. 5)
Weinberg, Steven 11, 66–67, 69, 72–73,
  73–74, 134n.11
Weisberg, Jacob 131n.17
Welte, Bernhard 135n.1 (ch. 5), 136n.9 (ch.
  5)
Will, George F. 131n.1
Witham, Larry 129n.3
Wolper, David 45
Woolf, Virginia 115
word *See* culture of the word

144